Exploring Greenland

*Twenty years of adventure mountaineering
in the great Arctic wilderness*

JIM GREGSON

East Greenland sunrise in Schweizerland

Exploring Greenland

*Twenty years of adventure mountaineering
in the great Arctic wilderness*

JIM GREGSON

Vertebrate Publishing, Sheffield
www.v-publishing.co.uk

EXPLORING GREENLAND
Jim Gregson

Vertebrate Publishing
Crescent House, 228 Psalter Lane, Sheffield, S11 8UT
www.v-publishing.co.uk

First published in 2012 by Vertebrate Publishing, an imprint of Vertebrate Graphics Ltd.

Photography by Jim Gregson unless noted otherwise.
Front cover photo: Peak Gymir, Saven Range.   Back cover photo: The peaks of central Paul Stern Land seen from Ararat.

This book is a work of non-fiction based on the life, experiences and recollections of Jim Gregson. The author has stated to the publishers that, except in such minor respects not affecting the substantial accuracy of the work, the contents of the book are true.

A CIP catalogue record for this book is available from the British Library.

ISBN 978-1-906148-09-6

Designed and typeset by Jane Beagley, in Avenir and Sabon, Vertebrate Graphics Ltd, Sheffield.
www.v-graphics.co.uk

Printed and bound in China by Latitude Press Ltd.

High peaks of the Pourquoi-pas Glacier

Greenland dawn

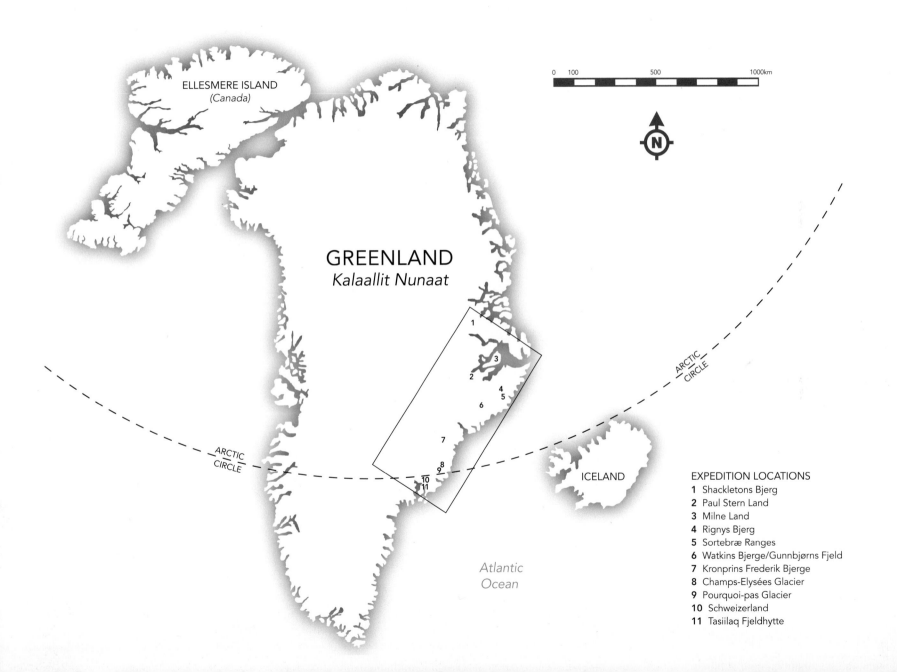

ELLESMERE ISLAND
(Canada)

GREENLAND
Kalaallit Nunaat

ARCTIC
CIRCLE

ARCTIC
CIRCLE

ICELAND

Atlantic
Ocean

0   100   500   1000km

N

EXPEDITION LOCATIONS

1   Shackletons Bjerg
2   Paul Stern Land
3   Milne Land
4   Rignys Bjerg
5   Sortebræ Ranges
6   Watkins Bjerge/Gunnbjørns Fjeld
7   Kronprins Frederik Bjerge
8   Champs-Elysées Glacier
9   Pourquoi-pas Glacier
10 Schweizerland
11 Tasiilaq Fjeldhytte

This book is dedicated to my wife, Sandra,
staunchest of companions.
With love

"To this day you can still hear people asking: What is the point of all these expeditions? What earthly use are they? Small minds, I always tell myself, have only time for thoughts of bread and butter."

Roald Amundsen, 1912

"Dreams are the touch stones of our characters. To be awake is to be alive. In wildness is the preservation of the world."

Henry David Thoreau

Table of contents

Foreword

Hooked upon a nail in my hearth at home, is a coiled eighteen foot Inuit sled dog whip made from a single strip of ringed seal hide. The place, and the moment in which I found it, represents a time in my life when a powerful need to explore wild Arctic regions had led me as a young man, to the epic east coast of Greenland. Our small manhauling expedition sallied forth in late June 1982 to make a crossing of the central ice cap of Greenland from the east to the west coast, one of only very few in the preceding hundred years since its first crossing by Norwegian biologist Fridtjof Nansen in 1888. The sled dog whip lay in the ground drift of spinning snow two kilometres from the rocky coast in a complex zone of crevasses; a discarded remnant, a tool of Greenlandic culture along the sparsely populated coast of Greenland, where travel by dog sled is a necessity for seasonal hunting parties.

This small find is a detail encountered within a vast landscape of wild territory where human activity is infrequent and rare. The elemental nature of Greenland's east coast of mountains and glaciers is too harsh for all but two small clusters of habitation; one being around Tasiilaq and Ittoqqortoormiit further north. Away from these places, to the north and east, are range upon range of alpine peaks extending from the coast to the edge of the inland icecap. It is to these most inaccessible mountain groups that exploration has developed slowly in the last century.

Traditional alpine mountaineering in Europe is crowded throughout the popular ranges of Oberland, Pennine Alps, Chamonix-Mont Blanc, and Dolomites. By the 1970s adventurers were seeking new horizons but access and cost were providing part of the barrier. The mountains of East Greenland remained utterly remote, largely unknown and inaccessible. For those prepared to forego the common precepts of 'adventure', Arctic mountaineering requires dedication into topographical research, acceptance of great hardships and desire for something that is real and committing. For those who do it, the rewards are rich: to enter a land of silent sentinel peaks, swathes of gigantic untravelled glaciers and an unearthly quality of light in a land so spare that one might feel as if they have abandoned the world and instead entered the flow of time. It is to this arctic fastness that Jim Gregson has dedicated more than twenty years of mountaineering exploration.

The Arctic has drawn him back time and again, whether it is to escape from the complexities of the world or the need to enter regular privations inherent during adventures into these remote icy mountains. Jim's recurring journeys back to North and East Greenland seem to be born from a simple desire to explore, not just the immense topography of remote ranges but to immerse himself in the details and wonders of the polar environment. Out there the land is implacable and harsh, but the detail is vibrantly interesting.

Throughout this lovely book, Jim Gregson brings us an acute vision of these textures in a quiet and engaging narrative, allowing us as readers, to find our own space of understanding within the vast expanses of this strangest of lands. He recounts details and observations with great clarity, like encounters with the many adapted animals and birds of high latitudes, the luminosity of light on the landscape, and insights into the lives of the Inuit communities surviving in a changing world. These pages

are 'the real deal' from an author hugely experienced in the rhythms and nuances of living in the outermost margins of the world.

Some of the exploits recounted in these pages are hair raising adventures of first ascents where the dangers of alpine mountaineering are clearly accentuated because of sheer remoteness, where radio signals are limited, and where skillful Arctic bush pilots provide the only link with the outside world. But Jim sees something more, he observes a sense of wonder about the Arctic, reflecting on its scale and its ineffable beauty, bringing us images of a wild place that few have ever witnessed.

Exploring Greenland is a clear historical and aesthetic record of mountain experiences in a rare and monumental landscape, delivered with the kind of humility experienced only by one who has ventured there. Encounters in these polar landscapes can change one's life, where the long hard hours on ski or in weather-bound camps are exchanged for memories and reflections of time well spent, and on this occasion shared with a generous and insightful spirit.

John Beatty

Making it Happen

Mountains mean a lot to me. But it wasn't always so. During my early teenage years I had a powerful interest in motorcycles and longed to own and ride one. My mother, not unsurprisingly, was not overly keen on me persisting with this wish. Perhaps she sighed with some relief when my energies were diverted towards birdwatching, camping and being in the outdoors.

Increasingly ambitious hiking trips, and the contents of the public library, directed me towards the mountains. Time in the hills made me aware of crags and climbers, and quietness. The pull of the motorcycle fell away. To her great credit, once I had intimated that I might have a go at some rock-climbing myself, my mother placed no object in my path.

From these acorns my lifelong involvement with mountains grew, and continues to flourish. After a progression through experience of British hills and mountains, summer and winter, including the stern schoolroom of Scottish winter climbing, I made the transition to the bigger challenges of the European Alps. The learning curve continued with the acceptance that to some extent in the Alps, improvements in technical competence must be accompanied by a certain willingness to suffer. Honest exercise indeed.

Eventually, realisation that expedition climbers were not really a special breed, more were they people who genuinely wanted to do it so much that they made it happen, then I decided to make it happen for myself. This led me to Greenland, and has kept on leading me there.

Jim Gregson

The Fox's Jaw cirque, Schweizerland, scene of high standard rock-climbing in recent years

1   Kulusuk Graves

The track from the airstrip to the village of Kap Dan on Kulusuk island wound across the tundra, sadly marked at intervals with discarded litter – rusted cans, odd pieces of machinery, beer bottles – contrasting strongly with cushions of jewel-bright flowers.

On a rocky rise stood two white-painted wooden crosses. Later we learned that here lay two victims of a polar bear attack. The trail breasted a slope from where the first dwellings came into view. Small wooden houses, with weathered but brightly hued paintwork.

Timber frameworks stood close by, hung with strips of drying fish and the darker, bloodied carcasses of seals. A few dogs tethered by chains sprawled by entrance steps, with here and there a litter of pups tugging at pieces of bone. Sledges and a few kayaks were off to one side.

Rounding a bend, a stripe of stronger colour foregrounded the main part of the settlement. Here was the cemetery. Graves headed with simple wooden crosses, paled through long exposure to intense sunlight, most of them bedecked with a cluster of flowers which on closer inspection proved to be artificial, made of plastic. There hardly seemed to be sufficient depth of earth to effect a burial here.

Beyond the graves, across the small harbour inlet, the homes of Kap Dan formed an irregular mosaic amongst the rocky knolls of a headland. Below them an assortment of small boats was haphazardly moored. By several buoys in the clear saltwater, clusters of seal corpses were fastened up in cold but wet storage. Children played on the boulders by the tideline edge. We were witnesses to a way of life different to our own.

Kap Dan village cemetery, Kulusuk

Weathered iceberg in Ammassalik Fjord

Pack ice in the sea near Kulusuk

2 A First Encounter with the Arctic

Schweizerland 1991

Being asked to step onto the weighing scales inside a small airline office at Reykjavik's Loftleidir Airport came as a bit of a surprise, heightening the sense of adventure for this, my first, expedition to Greenland.

Unlike the run-up to many climbing trips I'd made to the European Alps with much time spent poring over detailed maps and guidebooks, for this journey I'd had only one map, and that at a road map scale, and a few aerial photographs to study. Eager to see at first hand the wild Arctic towards which we travelled, with my three companions Paul, Brian and Simon, I boarded a little twin-turboprop aeroplane to fly from Iceland across the Denmark Strait to a gravel airstrip at Kulusuk, on a small island off the east coast of Greenland lying just south of the Arctic Circle.

Low cloud robbed us of any view during this flight, until suddenly we seemed to be flashing past snow-streaked mountainsides as the plane banked to land and snaked to a halt in the wet gravel. Hurrying to avoid the cold rain we rushed inside the prefabricated wooden building that in those days passed for a terminal. Here we were due to collect a consignment of kit freighted out in advance, spend one night in tents, then take a charter boat onwards to a landing place further north along the coast.

Two men approached us. "Are you the English group heading for Schweizerland?" one asked. "Yes, we are." "We have a boat ready, right now, if you're interested" said the other, naming a price. These two were Bengt Rodin, a Swedish adventurer and guide, and Peter Winter, an expatriate Dane, then resident in nearby Tasiilaq, the largest settlement in East Greenland. Paul, having handled our travel plans, was pushed forward to negotiate with these two characters while we three others sought warmer clothing from inside our rucksacks. The outcome of some haggling saw us within an hour buying fuel for our cooking stoves, climbing aboard a ramshackle pick-up truck and bumping down a track to a pontoon pier on the northwest side of the island.

Under a lowering sky we were chilled by a cold wind blowing rain across the ice-choked expanse of Ammassalik Fjord, with very little open water visible. While struggling to reconcile all this with the date, the last week of July, high summertime, we looked for the promised boat. The only craft in view was a grubby, cream-coloured fibreglass vessel such as one might see on a British canal or inland marina. Making a double-take over the chaotic and all too abundant pack ice, I found it hard to believe we had committed ourselves to a long journey in this cockleshell. Truly we were about to start an adventure.

Another friend of Winter's who served as a second steersman, plus a second Swede, Rodin's client, now appeared on the scene. That made eight bodies to cram into the little boat as well as the pile of expedition kit for six of them. Soon afterwards we cast off and the seemingly frail vessel nosed out from the pier and began to chug its slow way through the icefloes to head northeast along the fjords. The gloomy weather, too cold for staying out on the very limited deckspace for long, prevented us from seeing much more than the pack ice itself, backed by rock and scree slopes sweeping up into the low clinging cloud. Peter Winter, fortified by copious draughts of strong black coffee, estimated our journey time to be seven or eight hours, ice conditions permitting, for us to penetrate the upper reaches of Sermiligaq Fjord. The two Swedes were bound for a dropoff adjacent to the snout of the Knud Rasmussen Glacier some distance east of our own proposed landing.

On through the evening and into the night we motored slowly amongst the sea ice, with occasional manoeuvres to extricate the boat from dead-ends in the crowding floes. At times such an impasse would lead to someone having to clamber from the boat out onto the ice armed with a boathook to pole and push the vessel free. The grating and groaning of the rough ice against the thin-looking hull of the boat made a slightly scary impression on us in the half-light, reinforced by the sight of some true icebergs towering over us as we passed by. Sometime after midnight we closed up to the snout of the huge Knud Rasmussen Glacier stretched right across the fjord, several kilometres wide. Winter steered his boat to the east side of it, finally running it slowly alongside a wall of rock. Here, Rodin and his client scrambled out, jumping up onto ledges above the water then reaching down to drag up their equipment, manhandled across from the boat to them. With a few words and a wave we left them and steered away into the western arm of Sermiligaq where other glaciers debouched directly into saltwater. After another ninety minutes, the boat ran an arc round the massive floating end of an unnamed glacier and slowed to a halt in shallow water off a boulder beach.

A dinghy was launched and we were put ashore in the early hours, with enough light to see by filtering through the cloud cover. Standing by our pile of kit we watched as the tiny craft chugged away through the icefloes and disappeared from view beyond the snout of the enormous glacier pushing straight out into the sea. As the engine noise died away the remoteness of our situation bore down on us, isolated in the Arctic wilderness for the next four weeks. Somewhere up on the ice, 300 metres above the shore were our tents, skis and pulks (a sort of sledge) and 30 kilometres further inland was our main food and fuel dump, depoted by helicopter a few weeks earlier. Now we had to get up there ourselves. A first trip up the loose moraines and onto the ice itself took a few hours and we wearily pitched tents on the glacier and soon fell asleep. We had been on the move for more than thirty hours. Later in the day we descended to

the shore, making a cache of fuel and food for our eventual return, then relayed the rest of our gear back up to the tents. A few flowers grew on the hostile slopes of the moraine, and a thin-looking arctic fox scavenged round our camp for a while. Apart from ourselves these vestiges of life were the only variations in this world of rock, snow and ice.

The next day, refreshed by a good sleep, we loaded our pulks and harnessed up to begin the glacier trek inland to Slangen, a gateway pass to the mountains of Schweizerland. For July the snowline was low and soon we could step into our ski bindings and haul more easily. It was not so simple trying to grasp the scale of our surroundings: the glacier we ascended was wider and longer than any I had seen in the European Alps. Working up through the crevasses of an icefall we gradually rounded a big bend onto the undulating upper glacier stretching away from us for many kilometres. After six or seven hours of steady pulling we stopped to camp and eat, resorting to our sleeping bags as the temperature dropped to well below freezing point. The short night never grew properly dark, but the immense silence made a big impression on us. Another, shorter, day of hauling landed us at Slangen, a broad level pass with spectacular vistas of peaks to the north and flanked on both sides by interesting mountains. Good weather had now returned and having pitched the tents we spread our damp gear to dry quickly in the warm sunshine. Paul, exercising his flair for logistics (which I came to appreciate even more in the years to come) had arranged for a helicopter to drop off our main supply dump here at Slangen, which we soon located amongst the rocks to one side. The foodpile looked huge when we unpacked the boxes, but of course what you've forgotten you can't have. We sorted it into loads for outward and return legs of the trip. More weight to be moved, but we were buoyed to be in the heart of the mountains, and decided to do some climbing from here before moving further on.

Above our tents rose a fine rock peak, the walls of which were marked by an enormous intrusion or dyke writhing through the cliff – this was Slangen, Danish for "The Snake." We all felt drawn to this peak and eagerly packed climbing gear for an attempt via a ridge falling to the glacier a couple of kilometres down from the camp.

1

2

3

4

1 The author's very first Greenland glacier camp, Schweizerland   2 Schweizerland glacier travel mode   3 Tupilak summit catches early sunlight   4 Nearing the summit of P. 1720m

On the ridge we enjoyed a mix of snow and rock-climbing which led us up to the summit not long after midnight. Northwards lay literally hundreds of jagged peaks silhouetted against a purple and pink sky. The sun rotated just below this spiky horizon but it was light enough to find our way without torchlight for climbing and travel. Wanting to photograph my first Arctic sunrise, which would come into view in the north, I persuaded Paul, Brian and Simon to stay awhile on the summit. "It will be more comfortable than many a bivouac in the Alps" I told them. More than an hour passed and the sun was still reluctant to oblige so we decided to move off down. Reversing the ridge in the soft dawn light was a pleasant interlude of moving together as roped pairs, unhurried as we gazed around the vastness of our surroundings. Once back at the terrace where we'd left our skis we grinned at each other with satisfaction over our ascent, then skied contentedly up the firm glacier back to camp for breakfast, after which we fell asleep and woke some hours later roasting in the heat of the sun.

Now we planned to take food for two weeks and haul off northwards onto the 16 September Glacier to place ourselves amid the great cirque of peaks adjacent to the head of the gigantic Knud Rasmussen Glacier, to do some more climbing before retracing our way back through Slangen picking up more summits on our way back to the sea. Late one evening we left with bulky loads to ski down from Slangen, running in wide-radius curves and trying not to ski across the ropes linking us together. After two or three hours we realised that a mistbank rolling across the surface of the ice would soon envelop us, leaving us trying to navigate without landmarks. So we stopped and pitched the tents, luckily, as by midnight it began to rain which turned to sleet continuing for more than twelve hours. We spent the next afternoon and evening sleeping, reading, eating and sleeping again until the sky cleared and the temperature dropped sharply. A 4:30 am start got us away and over several kilometres of glacier to choose a campsite by an outlier of Tupilak, the area's highest peak, which is a huge twin-topped rock spire guarded by dangerous icefalls. By 9:00 we had our new camp set up and our wet stuff out drying. All around were splendid mountains, nearly all unclimbed, with all sorts of terrain on offer: ridges, big rock walls, icy couloirs, snow arêtes.

After scrambling up the rocky slopes above the tents for a few hundred metres to survey some possible lines for us to try, I was distracted then engrossed by the profusion of flowers growing on the gritty ledges – wonderful clumps of jewel-like colour, completing their astonishing lifecycles within the all too brief Greenland summer.

After a meal the next evening we slept till 10:30 pm then got up to ski over the hard glacier ice for an hour towards a fine peak facing our camp. Up a glacier bay then a gully, before a leftward traverse along ledges to a steep snow arête, we moved continuously together to cross a nice corniced crest just as the sun flooded its flank with golden dawn light. Behind us the summit spires of Tupilak flushed pink. Paul and I hung back letting Simon and Brian take pleasure in pushing out the route ahead. A short rocky scramble led onto the top where the view opened out east and north over ranks of pinnacled ridges and twisting glaciers, and far beyond, the iceberg-studded seas of the Denmark Strait. In the northwest the sky was a rich yellow and behind us the mountains glowed in the warm sunrise. We lingered in the calm air, shooting off copious amounts of film, drinking in the extensive panorama and sizing up some of the neighbouring tops. Eventually we descended without incident and skied happily back to the tents.

The following day we travelled west along the 16 September Glacier for a few kilometres beneath Tupilak, then climbed through some icefalls to approach the mountain lying directly above our camp. There was some interesting routefinding along the way until a final rock buttress gave onto a spacious summit. Even here we found a variety of flowers in bloom. Eighty kilometres inland we spied the bulky form of Mont Forel, long thought to be the second highest point in Greenland, and further to the west the plateau edge of the Inland Ice, the main icecap extending right across the island for hundreds of kilometres and up to 3,000 metres in thickness.

A short way to the north we could see another peak which attracted us. We studied a possible way of gaining access to its gleaming snow arêtes by a glacier arm and a steep ice tongue partly obscured by a minor rock buttress. We felt it would be worth a look. Once down through the icefalls, Brian and Simon, being less accomplished skiers, set off carefully down firm refrozen slopes. Shortly afterwards, Paul and I, despite the awkwardness of being roped together, managed a fall-free rapid descent by studiously synchronising our turns.

Resting in camp for a day gave us the chance to catch up on diaries and indulge ourselves with a wash and laundry session. To amuse the others I set to with shovel and snow saw and sculpted a fine seal replete with prunes for eyes. In the afternoon we unexpectedly spotted two tiny black specks coming down a distant glacier slope. In time these resolved into figures which approached our camp. They proved to be Bengt Rodin and his client on their lengthy tour. Over a drink of tea we heard how they had coped with an early mishap at the very start of their trek. When moving their gear from where the boat had put them ashore, they had relayed one set of loads up onto the Knud Rasmussen Glacier, leaving a depot by a large "mushroom" feature for easier relocation. While they went back for a second load, the mushroom, which is essentially a large boulder balanced on a plinth of ice, had collapsed and rolled over onto their kit, badly damaging their pulk and breaking one of Rodin's skis. With great difficulty they had retrieved a rope and ice axe and were eventually able to move the boulder enough to free their equipment. Despite the handicap of a weakened pulk and one ski broken across its centrepoint they had continued their long route but taking much more time than they had planned for. We had no spare ski to offer them as they settled into a bivouac near our tents for a few hours rest. They were still sleeping as we set out for our next climbing sortie.

A couple of hours of uncomfortable travel over sun-cupped, hard and gritty ice saw us climbing towards the ice tongue we thought would make a route up to the snow arêtes. As the slopes steepened we left the skis and cramponned upwards to where we could see the full extent of the tongue. Instead of the straightforward gradient we had expected this nearer view revealed to us a convoluted, serac-broken sweep of ice hemmed in by rocky spurs. I felt uneasy about this as we'd probably have to descend it later under a warming sun. Higher up we paused anew, trying to select a reasonable line. Suddenly, startling us, there was a sharp crack then a roar as blocks of ice crashed from a serac barrier and broke loose down the slope.

That decided us: we about turned very smartly and crunched off downwards to retrieve our skis. There were plenty of other mountains.

We opted to make our way back to Slangen, doing some more climbing on our coastbound journey, so set about dismantling our camp, leaving only footprints and ski tracks. By freak coincidence, as we recrossed the wide span of the 16 September Glacier we were again overtaken by a creeping fogbank which disorientated us for a while. When it cleared after an hour or so we looked back on our erratic zigzagging trail through ill-seen crevasse zones.

From Slangen we made two more fine ascents, one giving us the steepest ice pitches yet encountered to gain a footing on a corniced ridge leading to a summit tower of loose, rust-brown rock with room on top for only one person at a time. The other mountain route took us up through an icefall where progress was slowed by repair work on Simon's broken crampon. Despite this we continued along a succession of thin curling snow ridges poised high above the glaciers to finish on a rock turret. Myriad peaks receded away in all directions.

Having picked up our remaining food supply from Slangen we later left to head down to our shoreline rendezvous which Paul assured us he had fixed while at Kulusuk. Our speed of travel was now boosted by increased fitness and firmer snow surfaces, and we surprised ourselves by how rapidly we progressed down the glacier. We camped once more, hoping to fit in one more climb, but we were stalled when a sharp weather change unexpectedly pinned us down with a 24-hour snowstorm with high winds and zero visibility. After a second night we decided we'd try to move on come what may as we needed some time in hand to relay our loads down to sea level. The morning was brighter with some breaks in the cloud, so we dug out and packed to go. The soft new snow made the next few hours of pulling hard work, but in time we arrived at bare glacier ice. Soon afterwards we could no longer profitably use skis so we donned crampons for traction over the rough, stony lower reaches of the glacier.

Considerable melting had occurred while we had been inland and much snow had disappeared from these lower reaches. In places we had to manhandle the pulks through moraine bands and boulders, until a few kilometres from the sea we accepted that the time had come to carry everything. A drizzle fell as we stuffed our rucksacks, then strapped more awkward items onto the outsides. The loads grew to a point where we

Camp at Slangen Pass, Schweizerland

Ulimaut – the boat in Sermiligaq Fjord, Schweizerland

needed to help each other to pick them up. Stumbling and bent over, we struggled along the glacier edges and onto the steeply-falling lateral moraine to slip and slide our way down the 300 metres of descent to the shore. This was hard, hot, uncomfortable work until we sank with relief onto the boulder beach by the glacier snout. Our first notion had been to repitch the tents, sleep, then go back the next day for the remainder of our gear, but after some discussion we agreed to rest briefly then reascend to collect everything in one more trip. This would include the heavy ropes and climbing gear as well as the unwieldy pulks. Once it was all down we could fully relax. Grim-faced we toiled up the slopes one last time, realising how tired we were but committed to this labour. The second loads were immense, compounded by the pulks, nearly two metres long, lashed turtleshell fashion to our sacks. Four very weary climbers tottered down the shifting rubble to camp a few metres above the high tide level, grateful to be done with the worst physical hardship of the expedition.

The next day we sorted and packed almost everything into loads for freighting home, then savoured the splendour of our situation. Three enormous glaciers ran down from the mountains into Sermiligaq Fjord, with icebergs calving from their fronts at all hours of day and night, often in spectacular fashion only a few metres from our tents. Distant booms from across the sea were succeeded many minutes later by surging waves tossing the floating ice hither and thither. We walked along the water's edge and up the adjacent hillsides, absorbed by the colours and shapes of the ice in the sea, the textures of the rocks and the variety of flowers still in bloom late in August. The fjord head was filled with much more ice than had been present when we first landed and we wondered how our pick-up boat, due the next day, would cope. The hours of the following day slowly slipped by with no sign of the boat, but the fascinations of our environment made the extra stay easy to bear.

The sudden appearance of a red and white vessel nudging its way through the icefloes caught us unaware, making us scurry around to strike the tents and bundle away the last odds and ends. The *Ulimaut*, a very sturdy 12-metre converted fishing boat crafted in solid-looking timber could get no closer than 25 metres to the shore so we and our kit were ferried aboard by dinghy. The Greenlandic, Inuit people crewing the boat were very welcoming and soon we were under way bound for Kap Dan, 120 kilometres distant. The journey out through the fjords was a total contrast to our inward voyage, an eight-hour cruise of delight. The sun shone brightly from clear blue sky as we sailed past the high ice cliffs of the glacier snouts, moving between amazing icebergs huge and small, through narrow channels with mountainsides sweeping up directly out of the water. Iliviartik, Ikateq, Ilivinga, Ikasak – the names emphasising the "otherness" of our surroundings. We rejoiced in this moving kaleidoscope of visual experiences which lasted all day until the island of Kulusuk filled the view, still topped at that time by the alien aerials and radar scanners of its Distant Early Warning Station, a Cold War intrusion in a cold setting.

After landing we camped once more, this time on soft, yielding moss surrounded by nodding cotton grass. While waiting for a flight we took the opportunity to visit the Inuit people of Kap Dan village, Kulusuk's three hundred residents many of whom are still hunters. Their colourful wooden houses cling to the rocky ground in a superb setting, beautiful but no doubt not without some hardships due to its isolation. When our turn came to fly out to Iceland we stared over the cold ocean with lingering, longing memories of our fortunate time in the Arctic wilderness.

1991 BRITISH EAST GREENLAND EXPEDITION TO SCHWEIZERLAND, EAST GREENLAND
Paul Walker, Brian Povey, Simon Molyneux and Jim Gregson

Flying over sea ice

Descent from the Hutten Kogel, Schweizerland

Pack ice at Ikaasaartik, Kulusuk

3 Pack Ice

The floating pack ice in the ocean waters serves to emphasise the distinctive otherness of the Arctic. At times it presses a cold stillness onto this world of stone islands and abrupt mountain slopes jutting directly out of the fjords and inlets. But it can seem to come alive, waking from its inanimate state at the whim of wind or current.

When in motion the floes murmur and sussurate with the "growl" of the pack, audible at some distance or from vantage points at height. It is easy to grasp how this immense tonnage of frozen water governs access to the coasts of Greenland. Even large modern vessels must concede at times to the powerful natural forces exerted by ice and wave, outstripping the desires of men. Accounts of the former whale fishery attest to the dominance of the ice.

The Inuit, the people of East Greenland, have lived through the ages within this environment, not attempting to tame it or control it, but by evolutionary adaptation to the rhythms and conditions of the cold north. In contrast to the colourful contemporary wooden buildings of the present settlements, it is still possible to come across evidence of the former winter houses, some of which would have been in use within living memory. Drystone and sodwall enclosures, long abandoned, stand in close proximity to the tideline, mute witnesses to a way of life inseparably enmeshed with land, sea and ice for all sustenance. As ever was, the pack ice continues to drift by.

4 A Celebration on the Pourquoi-pas Glacier

Karabiner Mountaineering Club Greenland Expedition 1994

The trip into the mountains of Schweizerland acted on me like a catalyst and I longed to get back to the Arctic. I had enjoyed the vistas of ranked peaks spreading across the horizon in crystal-clear air, the silence of the glaciers, and the satisfaction of tracking untouched ground.

In my club, Manchester's Karabiner Mountaineering Club, there was talk of mounting an expedition to commemorate the club reaching its 50th year, due in 1994. This nub of an idea eventually focused down onto a proposal to get a team together to go to Greenland. There was a historical link: in 1960 John Hunt (of Everest fame) had been Honorary President of the KMC and had led that year an exploratory expedition to the Staunings Alper in Northeast Greenland, during which he had climbed and named a peak in honour of the club.

In the meantime, Paul Walker, my partner from the Schweizerland journey, had been out again making a long trek to climb Mont Forel: he was keen to go once more. From the KMC I was able to recruit Alan Jones, Graham Harkness, Andrew Howick and my wife Sandy. As plans firmed up we also invited another member of Paul's Forel team, John Starbuck, and a second female member, Lucy Derrick (soon after to become Paul's wife). Eight people would give us a good social mix with a reserve of manpower in the event of any mishap.

Research led us to choose to visit an area centred on the Pourquoi-pas Glacier, straddling the Arctic Circle just about midway between Mont Forel and Lake Fjord (Tugtilik), the place where Gino Watkins disappeared in 1932. Our plan involved flying in by ski-equipped aeroplane to land directly on the surface of the glacier: a new experience for us entailing the charter of a Twin Otter aircraft from Flugfélag Norðurlands in Iceland.

Loading this aeroplane with all of our kit and climbing aboard ourselves at the Kulusuk airstrip filled us with excitement. Once in the air we were glued to the cabin windows, gazing intently as the little machine skimmed across the fjords and glaciers, seeming to only just leapfrog the mountains en route. The pilot circled the proposed landing zone before deciding all was well and gently put the aircraft down onto the ice. Not so long after we'd unloaded everything he was powering up his engines and roaring off into the sky, leaving us standing amid a pile of boxes, rucksacks and skis with a promised pick-up date some weeks ahead. The silence of the white world crowded in on us, only thirty hours after leaving England. Heads whirling with impressions we fell eagerly to setting up camp, for some their first experience of camping on ice. Next day, after a short ski approach we climbed to a double-topped snow peak making a simple first ascent. We sat at the top using aerial photographs to orientate ourselves, identifying peaks and tentatively exchanging ideas for other possible camp placements to put us close to some enticing mountains we could see. We skied back to base with a sense of anticipated adventure for the days to come.

Packing for an eight-day sortie we depoted food and fuel against our return and on a cold evening we harnessed up the pulks to travel eastwards through the night hours. By midnight, in cool blue light, we pulled over a broad saddle from the Pourquoi-pas to look down across Seksstjernen (the Six Star), a vast confluence of six glaciers. In another thirty minutes we turned north then west to haul up a tributary glacier until we were placed below the north side of the mountains on the north bank of the Pourquoi-pas: here we camped.

High peaks at the eastern end of Pourquoi-pas Glacier

A superb peak for a first ascent

Sunrise from the north, over Sekstjernen

From this elevated location we climbed in the following nights and days seven more peaks and tops, all of them first ascents. This was a week of almost unalloyed pleasure, selecting routes by eye, employing ridge or face lines, enjoying our pioneering and sharing our pleasures. The best of these mountains was a noble pointed peak directly above our camp so we could approach it on foot, without skiing. A line through rock ribs took us towards its North East Ridge: a passage livened up for Alan by a broken crampon which had to be jury-rigged with a length of prusik cord pending a fuller repair later in camp. The crest of the ridge led arrow-straight to the summit, where our arrival coincided with a blazing re-emergence of the sun from behind a distant northerly mountain. There was no sense of urgency in our situation and we could relax on our new peak and take in the full circle view encompassing mountain, glacier, icecap and part-frozen ocean. We reflected on how distant we might be from other humans, and our good fortune in being able to experience this sense of isolation. After a safe descent to our tents we made more excursions, climbing and skiing to more mountains until we needed to return to base to re-supply.

As the move back onto the Pourquoi-pas was largely downhill we completed it relatively quickly and broke into our food depot. After a rest period we intended to make another foray to the east but were delayed by the onset of poor weather. At 1:00 am on the agreed date we found the sky leaden and mountains down the glacier to the west swathed in thick cloud. By 3:00 am snow started to fall and we were glad not to have set off. Rain or snow fell for two and a half days confining us to tents and sleeping bags: for some of us another learning experience in coexisting with the Arctic. The successes and pleasure of our first week sustained us through the long hours of inactivity while we waited for an improvement. When this came we watched as the sun gained ascendancy as cloud dispersed. We were surprised by a brief visitation from a group of strikingly white Ivory Gulls as we were such a long way inland from the coast: a reminder that there is a life presence here at times. We busied ourselves in drying damp belongings and revising our plans.

At the eastern end of the Pourquoi-pas Glacier we had noticed a group of impressive higher mountains, two of which in particular we felt would make good objectives – one a great fin of ice and rock, and the other a tall white pyramid. We needed to set a camp close to them, but first we'd have to get round behind some lower satellite peaks so decided on using an interim camp too. Accordingly we added to our pulk loads until we gauged we could allow for twelve days. This made the loads heavy to pull as we moved off one evening having waited for a fall in temperature to firm up the glacier surface. Heading past a prominent nunatak projecting from the ice we moved into the mouth of a sidebay of the glacier and by midnight we were pitching our tents. Still feeling the frustration from the storm-enforced idleness, John and I set off soon after to climb the nearest peak. This took us about two and a half hours first on a ridge of moss-decked rocks then steepening ice slopes leading to a snow dome. We followed a corniced edge to the highest point: just beyond on a rock shelf, sat a small cairn. On investigation the cairn held an aluminium canister containing a note left by the "Schweizer Groenland Expedition 1966" with two names appended. We added a note of our own before replacing it. At 3:30 am the sun rose as a bright red disk from behind high mountains at the far edge of Seksstjernen, flushing the landscape with colour. John and I took the chance to scout from this summit for access routes to the two target peaks we hoped to climb, noting glacier complications in the approaches of which our map made no hint. We also identified a suitable area for siting our next camp.

During the next night our whole group of eight was thwarted on an attempt on a big snowy mountain lying south of camp. The impasse which stopped us was in the form of a very deep and very wide bergschrund. This crevasse, invisible from below, cut across the whole slope for hundreds of metres without interruption. Despite traversing the mountain flank for half a kilometre or more we could find no way of forcing a crossing, so descended with some disappointment. On the way back to the tents we detoured to look into the huge "moat" surrounding the big nunatak, a spectacular feature, then enjoyed another powerful sunrise. This flattered to deceive as later in the day rain came on a west wind, turning to snow lasting into the next day. As it abated we discussed our situation, deciding to move nearer to the high peaks. In lovely evening light we hauled the pulks along the glacier below a row of subsidiary tops and icefalls until

Alpine style climbing in the Arctic

Storm clearance on Pourquoi-pas Glacier

we could turn uphill to go back west along a higher ice shelf to where we needed our camp. Having reached a suitable position in the middle of the night, we pitched our tents and slept soundly. Our chosen site had a sweeping view out across the whole of Seksstjernen and beyond towards the Inland Ice. As we were later to find out, this spot also caught the wind.

Cruelly, from 7:00 pm the next evening more rain fell, changing to snow which after twenty four hours lay as a cloak of deep powder. Now we needed to let this new snow settle, but tempted by the powder Sandy came with me very early in the morning to skin up the glacier in search of a suitable downhill slope. We cut a series of passable telemark turns into the new surface before returning to camp. Here we persuaded the others to come with us across the ice where we climbed one of the small rock peaks on the edge of the glacier shelf. This minor first ascent made our wait for settled conditions more bearable, boosting our spirits.

We felt ready for an attempt on the highest of our two target peaks, although Graham and Alan opted for some gentler exploration of their own. So, leaving them to go their independent way with a cautionary word about wariness of crevasses because of the recent snow, we remaining six made our way to an elevated col just below the final upthrust fin of our mountain. Having spent two hours reaching this col, we studied the way ahead: a steep ice slope cut by an obvious crevasse to a ridge punctuated by projecting rocks. Three ropelengths on 50 degree ice got us up onto the ridge where we used rock belay points for two more pitches up to the top most blocks at ca.2,400 metres, higher than any other summit in the vicinity. This good climb was rewarded with views from ocean to icecap with countless mountains pushing towards the sky. The descent went well and we skied back to camp in a happy mood. Alan and Graham arrived back contented too, having pioneered a pair of first ascents of their own. Now the big white pyramid beckoned strongly, a constant presence above our tents. Success here would send us back to base amply satisfied.

On the day decreed for this venture a fierce west wind roared over our tents and we postponed our start after a shouted discussion about windchill factors. Early in the following day when the sun ought to have brightened the scene we were still being blasted by spindrift, and snowdrifts were claiming our pulks. We calculated that six hours might

be needed for an ascent and waited another four hours hoping for some abatement in the wind. By the time a final decision became imperative, only Sandy and I were willing to commit to setting off, and we hurried to ready ourselves. The others agreed to wait for our return, knowing that we'd soon need to begin our return trek to base on the Pourquoi-pas.

Jostled by the cold rush of the wind, Sandy broke a trail away from the tents and we started our approach. Curiously, after not much more than fifteen minutes we reached the lee of the mountainside behind the camp and drew into stillness: calm air blessed us for the rest of the outing. Eventually we reached the limit of skiable progress then pushed on through deep snow on foot, making one long detour to bypass a massive crevasse. We were aiming to get onto the North Ridge of the mountain, a narrow arête firing up to the pyramid apex. After a cold stop to put on crampons we passed into a hollow filled with knee-deep powder to seek a crossing of the bergschrund arcing across the slope. By a deep blue gap we found a solid-looking snow bridge which would serve. We cut a knee step into the the upper wall, using it to gain a lodging on firmer ice above which delivered us onto the ridge. At this point we placed an ice screw and left a marker sling on it to guide our return. Dismayingly the ridge was loaded with windslab rather than the hoped-for névé on which we might have moved faster. Our crampons balled up badly and we laboured to gain height. After going over a corniced hump we reached a broader section of ridge where we even tried taking off our crampons. Higher up the crest narrowed again and we put them back on, but our pace was still slow. Aware of time passing we decided to leave our rucksacks before tackling the terminal crest.

First we climbed on the left side, then crossed to the right, the exposure becoming more and more apparent. The North East Face plunged down left in icy buttresses for six or seven hundred metres, and to the right the western flank was a sheer sweep of steep ice beneath our feet. We progressed on a short rope, with axe and hammer shafts driven into the very crest of the ridge, kicking hard to get our points through the soft top layers into the ice beneath. As this arête was not corniced we were constantly looking down the inhospitable northeast slope, but gradually we were closing on the top, where with a very slight easing we realised

Climbing high above Pourquoi-pas Glacier·

there was no more upwards to go. We were on the summit, just over four hours out from camp. Far, far below we could see the others out on the ice: we yelled our arrival but the sound was blown into the ether. They had seen us, we later learned, but were still anxious over our descent.

And anxious also were the two of us, realising that our experience of Alpine terrain would be severely tested on the way down. Security would lie in mutual trust as much as anything else. Having kicked good footings into the ridge flank, the first narrow section was not too bad apart from a few collapsing steps. After we'd picked up our sacks things got more wearing. Every so often the snow settled with sickening creaks and we struggled with our balled-up crampons. Minor slides broke away from our feet giving us a few heart-in-mouth moments. Recrossing the corniced hump was particularly nerve wracking and we arrived at the ice screw marker in a state of considerable tension. The screw had loosened due to some melt-out so had to be re-positioned and backed up with a second one. Sandy climbed down carefully to prod the snow bridge in the bergschrund and cross over it gingerly before securing a sound anchor beyond. I followed down in turn, treading as lightly as possible onto the softened folds then stepping wide onto safer ground. We were heartily relieved to be off the hazardous snow of the arête and embraced with a few shudders. Removing crampons we plodded through the now wet afternoon snow to our skis and pushed them slowly downhill towards the tents and the ready congratulations of our friends. They had kindly prepared drinks and a meal for us, but soon we needed to sleep for a while at least.

After just a few hours they gently roused us to join them for the return journey through the night hours. This was not always the carefree skiing we'd enjoyed earlier. Descending with loaded pulks we found ourselves in snow where only running step turns would work, and catching an edge I took a heavy twisting fall. The impact from this tumble caused my pulk towbar to break free from its mounting while the liberated pulk careered off on its own down the glacier, leaving me in a heap on the ice. Pursued by Andrew and Graham the pulk finally ground to a halt after more than half a kilometre, thankfully without finding any crevasses. John and Graham, the engineers, set to to make repairs before we could resume our travel. With increased weariness we covered the last kilometres back to base camp, arriving in the early hours. Restorative sleep preceded our packing and re-organisation for the pick-up flight. However, even in this waiting period, John and Andrew found energy to climb one more mountain on which they found evidence of nesting sites for the Ivory Gulls, while Alan and Graham made a final tour in search of flowers. The rest of us savoured the peace of our temporary glacier home, reflecting on our fine experiences and shared endeavours.

The arrival of the Twin Otter broke the quietude of the Pourquoi-pas Glacier but the flight out to Kulusuk was an impressive finale to our expedition, reinforcing my affection for these Arctic wilds. The "once in a lifetime" had been repeated. Perhaps this was the firm establishment of a love affair, and I would soon seek another assignation with this suitor in the north?

1994 KARABINER MOUNTAINEERING CLUB GREENLAND EXPEDITION
Jim Gregson (Leader), Sandy Gregson, Graham Harkness, Andrew Howick, Alan Jones, Paul Walker, Lucy Derrick, John Starbuck

This expedition was fortunate to have the support and grant aid of the Mount Everest Foundation, the British Mountaineering Council and the Gino Watkins Memorial Fund. The Lord Hunt of Llanfair Waterdine was also our encouraging Patron.

4:00 am near Camp 2 on Pourquoi-pas Glacier

Camp 3 below P.2370m

Ammassalik Fjord from Kulusuk

From the mountains to the sea in the Denmark Strait

Major crevasse zone in the Kronprins Frederik Bjerge

5   Silence of the Land

Two sensations embed themselves into your consciousness when you venture into the wild Arctic. Coldness and whiteness might come immediately to mind, but these are not for me the things that most command attention. On all my journeyings in Greenland's fastnesses, I have always felt more aware of the silence of this northern land, coupled with a sense of space: a keen realisation of the vastness of unknown, untravelled, uninhabited territory, reminding you of your own smallness.

For some people perhaps, true silence may seem unnerving, even disturbing. But for me it has usually been reassuring, calming, conducive to a feeling of peace and well-being. Of course, there is not, even in the Arctic, a total absence of sound at all times. Running water, snowfall or spindrift meeting tent fabric, wind, falling rocks, cracking ice, all add at times to the experience of being in these northerly regions and camp life with one's own group of companions produces its own soundscape behind time spent here. Often though, there are periods of quietude when all sound recedes until the solitude of true silence reigns, settling onto the landscape and its temporary residents. The rarity of this in our normal lives and surroundings heightens the acuteness of ones awareness and appreciation of it in these situations of genuine wilderness. To me it is one of the treasures of fortunate time spent in these special places, almost a healing process as you allow yourself to be absorbed into the quietude.

The sheer scale of the Arctic environment brings the second, almost tangible sensation. Here the landscape is vast, immense across one's field of vision. Even amongst innumerable jagged peaks and mountain ranges massed before your eyes, the overwhelming realisation is one of the surface of the planet extending into distances beyond imagination. This gives a powerful sense of your own tininess: you are manifestly a minute speck in nature. Here, man is not the measure of things. Here we are visitors, guests, privileged specially to be the first to make footprints on untrodden ground. Thus in a way it is fitting that we should feel small in such surroundings. Any significance lies not "in" us, but our very being there is significant "to" us, for not everyone is granted the particular favour of reaching somewhere for the very first time.

6   At the Edge of the Inland Ice

A summer in the Kronprins Frederik Bjerge 1996

"How would you like to come out for the whole summer?" Paul asked me. He was planning a lengthy trip to explore and climb in the long remote chain of mountains called the Kronprins Frederik Bjerge. These ranges stretched for hundreds of kilometres along the fringe of the Inland Ice, Greenland's central icecap, from latitude 67 to 69 degrees North. They had been seen by Martin Lindsay's sledging party in 1934 but perhaps by only two or three small groups since then.

As Paul had put together a larger group of people for this venture it took some days for the first contingent to gather at Kulusuk. A transformation had occurred there since my previous visit: the ramshackle airport buildings had been replaced by a much larger, ultramodern terminal, its sleek structural lines looking slightly alien to its age-old surroundings: a sign of increasing change of pace for this Arctic gateway. I had a pang or two of nostalgia for the old wooden sheds, the beaten-up rusty fire truck and the ancient wrecked aeroplane by the far end of the runway.

During the waiting days until everyone arrived we installed a camp by a stream on a zone of yielding moss not far from the airstrip. The fjords and sea channels were clogged and crowded with icefloes and bergs. Boat movements were severely hampered and we were glad that our onward travel would be airborne. In the meantime we enjoyed walking and scrambling around the island seeking out attractive flowers and colourful lichens. We took pleasure in watching snow buntings, wheatears, ringed plovers and on one occasion a magnificent slow-flying, low-flying Gyrfalcon. Our camp was also visited frequently by an Arctic Fox scavenging for scraps. This creature, increasingly bold, would even at times accompany us for parts of our walks.

Above our camp and the airstrip a gravel road led up into the hills past a number of small lakes. This road had once served the former US base and DEW-Line early warning radar station which had still been in operation in 1991. Since then the Cold War thaw had resulted in its dismantling and removal. Out of curiosity, Paul, Lucy, Sandy and I took a walk up there one day, finding only a tall radio relay mast and a small locked cabin by a helicopter pad. Completely gone were all the radar domes and listening apparatus, the buildings, perimeter fencing and armed guardposts: the only visible remnants were concrete foundations on which everything had stood. Here was clear evidence of the peace dividends achieved in the Reagan-Gorbachev period. From this and other high points we could stare out beyond Kap Dan over the chill blue waters of the Denmark Strait, listening to the "growl" of the pack ice as it responded to the motions induced by wind and wave.

When all of our team was assembled we could organise the two flights of the Twin Otter which would be necessary to lift us all 200 kilometres northwest. Going in on the first flight I was able to recognise those glaciers and peaks I'd visited during my previous journeys, then looked eagerly ahead as we neared the increasingly white world of the high territory bounding the vast icecap. The aeroplane circled over a high wide saddle before the pilot slid it gently to earth at an altitude of 2,500 metres. We stepped out into deep snow and quickly offloaded our equipment, allowing the crew to go back to Kulusuk to fetch our other companions. By the time the second flight came in we had some tents in place, and began to have a clear sense of the sheer coldness of our elevated location.

Anniversary Peak – the final moves of the first ascent

The wind roars over Anniversary Peak during the first ascent

1 Storm day at Kronprins Frederik Base Camp   2 Moon over storm-hit Kronprins Frederik Base camp

We said our goodbyes to the aircrew who would return after three weeks to permit an exchange of personnel as not everyone was able to stay for the whole of summer. After the engine noise died away and the aeroplane was lost to view we felt that special silence of the Arctic, a pointed reminder of the remoteness of our situation and for first-timers always an impressive moment. We busied ourselves with setting our camp in order, spurred by the bone-penetrating windchill insistently reminding us of its origin in air spilling off the icecap, catching out those unwary enough to handle metal with ungloved fingers.

The long months of planning, preparation and anticipation had made us eager for action and we could all see tempting objectives. Our map was three-quarters blank of detail, representing the immensity of the icecap stretching away from us: interestingly our aerial photographs showed mountain peaks in places where the map remained empty. Frustratingly, our early forays were sporadic as we were beset by a period of disturbed weather, typically two days good followed by two days bad. Nevertheless we were able to make a number of climbs and ski journeys, delighted to be the first people tracking this ground. Storms and high winds dumped snow onto us, reinforcing our isolation in this cold place, and in calmer periods we could observe those eerie phenomena known as parhelia or sundogs. These give the illusion of three suns visible at once in the sky, caused by light refracting through ice crystals suspended in the air. Our camp area was soon deeply drifted and much energy was spent in shovelling snow away from the tents. It was not long before we had shovelled ourselves into a white-walled labyrinth of passageways and we had to resort to clear waymarking of the track to the latrine. Such weather spells are testing times for patience and group morale but our opportunistic outings led to firmer plans being laid.

After a week we split into three smaller parties, each one choosing a new area in which to travel and explore. For a few this would prove to be a baptism by toil as new-fallen snow makes pulk-hauling with heavy loads an arduous business. With Lucy and Paul, Sandy and I decided to go out westwards to get amongst a group of free-standing peaks on the very edge of the Inland Ice, drawn by the prospect of experiencing this great horizontal whiteness. First though, as others packed loads, we set our sights on a mountain lying east of our base which might furnish us with a lofty view over to the icecap. The ascent of this mountain went slanting up and across hard, wind-carved snow to a ridge where huge seracs hung over a deep, deep drop into the next glacier valley. With care we found a route to the highest point from where we could gaze all round. Away to the northeast several high mountains held plenty of promise for later on, and we were excited by the icecap edge peaks we were heading for the next day. As we came down to our skis we were surprised to see a lone figure come into view. This proved to be Toby, our team doctor, who had at short notice chosen not to go off with either of the other two groups, so we enrolled him into ours.

The next day we assembled and packed all we needed and hauled off slowly towards the icecap, passing close to one massively imposing peak which lodged itself firmly on my wish list. But for now we were headed further out and pressed forward for some more kilometres until we could place a camp at the foot of a good-looking mountain. Over the next few days we climbed to this peak and three others as ski ascents. Each gave us the opportunity to stare over the wide space of the Inland Ice, unrolling featureless away from us to a gently curving horizon at a distance impossible for us to quantify. We even made time for a reconnaissance trip towards the big peak I had taken to calling the "Crown Prince" in the hope of a later attempt. For now, though, the weather intervened again and we were back in the waiting game while fresh snow fell and blew around us, obliterating all our tracks radiating from this camp. We read and slept the hours down, hoping for a prompt return to stable conditions. Paul, conscious of the approaching date for the midpoint pick-up when some team change was due, indicated that in another day we'd need to tackle the journey back to base camp. We had been tentbound throughout a long weekend but steeled ourselves to return the next day.

Our luck was still out in the morning but we set to and dismantled the camp in spite of a strong northeast wind, and soon after 10:30 am we bent into our pulk harnesses. Once under way breaking trail was very arduous, as the days of poor weather had produced a thick blanket of new snow. Ski tips refused to float and often a forward push merely buried them deeper as the heavy pulks settled and were reluctant to glide.

For the man or woman in front there was the added problem of nothing to focus vision on, whereas the followers could at least see the struggles of those ahead. Each of us took turns out in the lead, with Paul and myself double-checking the team with compass bearings, but our slow pace probably didn't exceed one kilometre per hour. As a further check on progress Paul was using a GPS receiver, new to us at that time, so although we had no respite from the unrelenting white-out in a visual sense, we were able to reassure ourselves that we were in fact creeping closer and closer to base camp. Midday came and went, long before the halfway distance but we stuck to our task, not really wanting to reset our camp. The final kilometres were uphill and we found ourselves going on into the evening hours, muscles aching and eyes straining. Even in a group as we were, travel like this is a lonely business: each person must make his own effort and apart from halts there is little opportunity for collective support or conversation.

Nonetheless we continued, and at last the dark shapes of tents softly emerged from the greying gloom. This meant, of course, that the other teams were back in residence, even though our yells and whistle blasts had gone unanswered. In time a single figure appeared, then others quickly after and we finally pulled into camp to a chorus of greetings. Our friends had not imagined that we we'd try to travel on such a poor day but soon had hot drinks ready, with willing hands to help us pitch our tents. This demanding trip had taken more than ten hours to complete, physically and mentally tiring, but satisfying confirmation that our navigation skills were reliable. Tomorrow would be soon enough to catch up on everyone's news.

That tomorrow was also plagued by poor weather so there was little prospect of the expected flight coming in. The other groups had had varied fortunes: some good peaks were climbed, others proved elusive. For the younger climbers the last week was a deep learning experience – one of them had suffered painfully frostnipped feet enforcing prolonged rest. More significantly, more people than anticipated had decided that they'd had enough of bad weather and were set on going home when the ski-plane came. In the morning of the next day we eventually heard the engine drone from the Twin Otter. As the aircraft circled the camp Paul advised the pilot by radio about a heading for landing relative to the massive snowfall and wind direction since we had all arrived. When the plane touched down the ski undercarriage was immediately lost to view and the whole machine shuddered and bucked its way under power up towards the tents. Five new arrivals pulled their kit out onto the snow, and the seven now leaving loaded theirs in turn. We spent a little time with the pilots getting an update on weather information before they told us they'd have to go. The take-off was not so straightforward because of the depth of snow. A couple of very long taxi runs were made up and down to extend the track before a full throttle charge finally dragged the Twin Otter off the saddle and into the air, with a turn over the tents for a farewell buzz then heading south until lost to our sight and hearing. One great bonus from the flight which we particularly appreciated was the delivery of a box of fresh potatoes and apples which varied our menus for some days. Of the newcomers, four aimed to head south in search of new ground and rejoin us later for pick-up. Tom joined the first small group along with Toby, Mike and Anne-Marie, while we, the two married couples reverted to our original team of four.

Still recovering a little from our icecap trek, we spent an unladen day making some ski ascents and spying out the terrain over to the northeast where we intended to journey. While we were thus engaged the other two parties left base with their supplies. The next day, mid-August, Sandy, Lucy, Paul and I loaded sacks and pulks and travelled away from base camp with the intention of getting over into the next large glacier basin where we had noticed some very fine mountains. En route we passed through the interim camp of Mike's group: they were away busying themselves with some mountains out to the west. We continued on our way gradually losing height until we chose to camp in a location which would allow access to a wide choice of untouched mountains. Although by now we were some 500 metres lower down than base camp, the cold was intensified by airspill off the icecap and we worked quickly to set up our tents and create shelter.

Immediately before us lay a wonderful mountain, our target for tomorrow. That day would be a wedding anniversary for Sandy and me, so the choice of name for this peak in the event of a successful first ascent was not going to be too imaginative, although perhaps a little romantic.

A magnificent first ascent traversed the nearest two peaks, MP2480 and WE2470

Climbing the East Ridge of WE2470

By 6:00 am we were away from the tents after a very chilly breakfast time, skiing up to reach the mountain's North West Ridge. As we fitted crampons to our boots we could see long banners of spindrift streaming off the cornices high on the arête, and as we gained height our ropes blew out in taut arcs between us. Finely positioned but without excessive difficulty, the arête led us up to the summit, guarded by cornices, and we were indeed happily successful on this, our Anniversary Peak. After an hour of retracing our steps downwards we met Toby and Mike from the other party who had made a long ski approach to reach this peak before repeating our ascent. We made an agreement to combine the two groups for an attempt on the other big peak in the vicinity, after they moved over to our camp in another day or so.

A night of howling wind and driving spindrift found us only slowly getting into gear the next morning, clearing deep drifts from the tents. In time we set off towards the south, struggling to cross some fields of sastrugi to gain footing on the end peak of a beckoning ridge. We climbed a steep crest to a first summit and while stopped, noticed the four figures from the other group arrive at our camp. The ridgeline continued to further peaks so we embarked on a high-level traverse which took us over two more summits on very interesting ground, with many more mountains in view and way out to the east the blue of the ocean dotted with icebergs and pack ice. Days like this one give that special satisfaction of knowing you are the first (and maybe the last?) to make footprints along this crest, with the extra spice for a climber of not knowing in advance what problems the mountain might present. Our return to camp was joyous and in company with the others we outlined a plan for the next day.

Now there were eight of us at the same camp and we would join forces to climb a significant peak together. Paul, however, tempted us with a variant start by an ascent to an outlying summit then traversing a sharp arête to link back to the main mountain. Mike's group chose to aim directly for this latter but would wait for us at the intersection. So it was as the two couples again that we left camp early to ski out towards the mountain, negotiating some zones of very awkward snow on the glacier, badly cut about by the recent fierce winds. A steep slope of ice had to be climbed to get onto a narrow crest which we followed to a rocky summit: then a descent and reascent along a very delicate and attenuated arête saw us rejoin our waiting friends to complete the climb to the main summit. The final section was marked by a gigantic cornice projecting several metres out into the air, demanding a wide berth before we all gathered at the top, wreathed in smiles at our happy circumstance in just being in such a wonderful location. Far off in the north lay the highest Arctic peaks of the Watkins Bjerge, identified only in the 1930s: out to the east the ice-pocked waters of the Denmark Strait: in the west the enormous stretch of the crevasse-patterned Inland Ice, and all around, closer to hand, the myriad summits of the Kronprins Frederik Bjerge where we had travelled and climbed in the preceding weeks. Cheered by our good fortune we returned to camp.

After a rest day we went off to the south, where a string of summits seemed to offer the chance of another traverse. From the first top a series of rock towers stretched along the crest with the promise of intricate routefinding. Paul and Lucy opted out of this in favour of another mountain further along the glacier so Sandy and I moved into the towers. Not so straightforward now, some ups and downs brought us to tricky ground and a big rock step. Neither left side or direct would go, but exposed moves right led with difficulty into a corner groove where rotten snow had to be hacked away to uncover rock holds. Higher, a great block of rock was passed on the right where a ledge led to a second groove at the top of which was a small platform. Here we had to take off our crampons to deal with more complex rock moves for some distance, but in time the way to the next summit became clear and we were a little surprised to see that our watches showed that almost four hours had slipped by. Beyond this point the rocky ground gave way to snow and ice ridges so we decided to continue to one further prominent summit, completing another hat-trick outing. We were then able to force a descent on the north flank to regain our footing on the glacier below, leaving an easy though wearying flog back to our skis. Spotting Lucy and Paul on their own return at the far side of the glacier assured us that all was well and when we had all gathered at the tents we shared our experiences through the evening.

Treading a fine line on MP2480, a first ascent traverse over three peaks

There was another parting the next morning when the four in Mike's group left to explore further to the south again. The day after, we ourselves packed up to return to base by travelling up and along another untrodden glacier. The surface conditions favoured us and we were able to maintain a good pace, with only one long taxing gradient which forced us into a left-leading diagonal calling for a big effort. These days of pulk hauling were the price we paid for our magical climbing outings so the discipline had to be endured, somewhat relieved by the splendid surroundings. In the afternoon we skied the last kilometre across the saddle of base camp to a changed scene. The depot of food was well drifted up and because of the winds in the last week the deep aircraft track was barely visible. For our final few days stay we reset our tents a short way down from where they'd been before, knowing that all the others would home in on them as they too made the pick-up rendezvous. Time remained for us still to make some climbs, one of which was the small peak immediately above the camp location. From its top we could see the base in birds-eye view as the hub for all our journeys and it was pleasing to pick out all the places we had visited. My eye was particularly drawn to the massive form of the Crown Prince, the dominant mountain of the area. It would be a shame not to make at least an attempt on it.

Back at camp, Paul would not be persuaded so Sandy and I resolved to try as a pair. The distance to the peak would mean having to make a genuine Alpine start so we readied all our equipment and retreated to our sleeping bags. 2:30 am arrived and we shivered into activity, frost crystals showering from the tent fabric as we moved about. By 4:00 am as we stepped into our ski bindings, the eastern sky glowed orange and red as the sun breached the horizon and we pulled away from camp. Still it took us almost three hours to reach the attack point for the West Ridge of the mountain where in calm air we fixed our crampons. A hundred metres of slope put us up on the ridge, looking down into a much bigger drop on the icecap side. Moving together we turned up the crest, forced onto its northern side by the corniced rim. As the ridge reared up so its flank steepened and we found ourselves on 55 degree slopes, kicking hard to try to make sound footing. All the weather vagaries of the last weeks had combined to cloak the mountain in swathes of windslab or sugar snow, in places lying one over the other, calling for great care. Poised above a huge swooping north flank dropping from our heels we could see cones of avalanche debris trailing out onto the icefields far below, and great expanses of scoured blue ice where they had their source. This was so different from the other mountains and climbs we'd accomplished in recent weeks.

After a couple of hours we crested a minor rise and stopped in awe of the forward prospect: a long section of ridge topped by an edge of undulating cornice of incredible thin-ness, the flank a gigantic sweep of blue ice, and further on a pronounced dip from which the final arête soared away up to the summit. Caution, judgement, fear most definitely – whatever, we decided that for us on this day the risk of continuing was too great and we reluctantly turned to descend. Even this called for great concentration as we carefully retraced our steps. On reaching our skis we reassured ourselves that our judgement and decision had been the right ones to make in the light of conditions, and we set off to go back to base feeling that at least we'd made an honest try. A very fine prize awaits future suitors. Paul and Lucy greeted us at the tents after our twelve-hour excursion, later inviting us to join them for a final outing the next day.

In the morning we all skied away, dropping into a branch glacier to the west to run along below a line of mountains which did not show on our maps. Paul had spotted an attractive summit a few kilometres along this line and led us to its foot. By ice slopes and a short section of rock we climbed to a forepeak, looking across a dip to the highest point linked by a fragile-looking snow arête. Crossing this to the actual summit gave precisely two rope lengths of delicate work before our final descent in softened snow to the skis. Paul now forged a track across the glacier to take us back to base by a new route over a pass to complete a long circular tour of genuine off-map exploration. Tired as we were on arriving at the camp, we were very happy as our long summer was reaching its final days.

During the afternoon of the following day, a Monday, Paul called our attention to the small specks of one of the other groups making their way back towards base, and by coincidence, while they repitched their tents the final four also hove into sight, so by early evening the camp held a complement of twelve, a veritable village. We exchanged news

The still-unclimbed Crown Prince peak at the edge of the Inland Ice – camp visible to the right

of our various travels and climbs and began to anticipate our return to "normal" surroundings. Tuesday passed in sessions of sorting and packing equipment with our pick-up flight expected on Wednesday. The weather on that day let us down once more and as the hours passed by we came to accept that the aeroplane might not arrive. By chance Paul was able to make radio contact with a high altitude commercial airliner flying over and by relaying messages we eventually learned that our skiplane was still in Iceland awaiting better weather conditions down at Kulusuk. Direct contact was beyond the range of the radio set we had. Thursday came and we rekindled our hopes but the weather clamped down again. Further relayed radio messaging was made and we were informed that our aeroplane was heading for Kulusuk, but we were dismayed by the arrival of freezing fog then snow. For some people the waiting was beginning to pall, compounded by the prospect of missing final flights home, but in the Arctic the weather rules and one must go with it rather than rail in vain.

Friday turned into another day of frustration as the conditions were still against us, and some in the party found this a sore trial of patience as we felt hemmed in by the cold grey fog. The joyous days of climbing in crisp sunshine seemed to have receded so quickly. However, nothing we could do or say could influence matters materially. Saturday dawned with sunlight and spirits began to revive. Before 9:00 am we suddenly became aware of engine noise and to our pleasant surprise and relief the Twin Otter flashed into view and landed in a trice. As we rushed to strike the tents and pack the last items, the pilot ploughed his "runway" up and down before running up to a halt. When he stepped down, his face was unfamiliar to us but he obviously meant business. He told us that he'd already tried to come in the previous day but had turned back due to the fog choking our base area, but now he proposed to overload the Twin Otter and try to get all of us out in one lift as the weather was not wholly reliable. To this end the aeroplane had been stripped of all seats and surplus fittings and would be stuffed with all of our equipment and we'd just have to wedge ourselves in there with it! If the plane wouldn't make the take-off, then some of us would have to be offloaded with our kit and take another wait. Some of the group were so appalled at this prospect that Sandy and I volunteered, to ease the situation.

The take-off run was an adventure all in itself. Once throttled up the aircraft careered across the ice struggling to accelerate, bucking wildly as it passed the end of the prepared track. There was a frightening dropping feeling as the glacier slope steepened in gradient and there were a lot of white knuckles as the pilot fired it down the hill. Suddenly the aeroplane skis sucked themselves clear of the surface and we felt the lift kick as the machine pulled itself into the thin air. Raucous cheers burst from relieved faces and dry throats: we were on our way home!

1996 14 JULY - 3 SEPTEMBER, EXPEDITION TO THE KRONPRINS FREDERIK BJERGE, EAST GREENLAND
Paul Walker, Ralph Atkinson, Andrew Robertson, Lucy Walker, Steve Girt, Harriette Purchas, Jim Gregson, Steve Houghton, Edward Watson, Sandy Gregson, Humphrey Deman, Martin Lodge, Anne-Marie Nuttall, Mark Thrush, Mike Fletcher, Craig Cook, Dr Toby Richards, Paul Endersby and Tom Keely

Avoiding the cornices during the first ascent of WP2520

Icecap edge camp in the Kronprins Frederik Bjerge

Skiing to the south of Crown Prince,
Kronprins Frederik Bjerge

Arctic Fox Photo: Dmitry Deshevykh

7 Volpone – Issittup Terriania

Snow Buntings often flitted about by the little cluster of tents pitched on the tundra. Their contact calls could be heard, overlaying the gurgle and chatter of the nearby stream. During the days we spent here, we learned to recognise the changed notes which signified the buntings' warning or alarm call.

This usually indicated the appearance of an Arctic Fox, foraging across its island territory and frequently visiting our camp in the hope of scavenging scraps to eat. As the days of our weather enforced stay succeeded each other the fox became a regular, with increasing boldness. It would nose among the cooking pots, tug at the tent guylines, and creep up close behind anyone bent on cleaning duties at the bank of the stream.

We were, of course, seeing this animal in its summer pelage, grey-brown above with paler flanks and underbelly and a lighter coloured tail. It wasn't difficult though, to recognise how well-adapted the Arctic Fox is to the harsh northern climate. The ears, muzzle and legs are fairly small, while the tail is large and bushy. The gaze of the golden or orange-yellow eyes is direct and strong. As winter approached the fox would grow its white cold weather coat with long guard hair overlying a thick and dense underlayer. making itself look much larger. In times past this transformation made the Arctic Fox one of the prime targets for fur trappers.

Not far from camp I had found a long whip, bound onto a wooden shaft, discarded or lost by an Inuit dog-sledge driver. With gentle flicks of this whip it was possible to entice our vulpine visitor into a game, where the fox would creep, stalk and pounce at the ragged ends of fibres. If it was successful in catching the strand ends, the lively creature would engage in a gentle tug-of-war.

Amazingly, the fox could be induced to follow for some distance by trailing the whip along the ground. We had some equipment stored in a container adjacent to the nearby airstrip buildings, perhaps two hundred metres away. Needing to access some of this kit, I found I could tempt the fox to accompany me for most of the way, but twenty five metres short of the buildings the fox would stop and lie down. I went on and entered the bulding. When I came back outside to return to camp after ten or fifteen minutes the fox was still there waiting, and trotted all the way back keeping me company at a distance of only two or three metres.

In traditional tales, the Arctic Fox often appears as a shape-shifter or trickster. Here we saw a wild creature transform itself into a playful companion, at least for a short interlude in its life.

8 Paradise Lost then Found

Champs-Elysées Glacier 1997

Weather systems won out over aviation technology at the start of this venture. For two days we couldn't get across from Iceland to Greenland until a short break in cloud cover got us transferred to Kulusuk, where we placed our tents by a stream crossing the tundra below the airstrip. The island had less snow that year, but the mosses, flowers and grass seemed less advanced.

The days continued to be marked by rain and low cloud, just allowing a few flights to arrive and depart. There were a number of groups that summer, all relying on a shuttle schedule involving the ski-plane to place them into their respective destinations in the mountains. The encampments grew – French, Norwegian and British contingents lending a cosmopolitan air to the surroundings, and there was an interesting international bonhomie round the driftwood campfire. But as the days wore on with no breaks or improvement in the weather frustrations sapped at morale. We could explore further on Kulusuk island itself, and spent some time seeking out former Inuit settlement sites away from the current village area. Sod and stone walls marked abandoned earlier dwellings barely above the high tide line, and burial cairns occupied knolls of higher ground. Another day saw us making a climb to the top of Qalorujoorneq, highest point on the island, where we huddled from cold, wet winds pressing grey cloud onto the mainland mountains.

The gloomy mood was not helped by the eventual news that the time window for the ski-plane flights had closed as the air company was contracted to other business elsewhere. Ten days of our time had been lost to this delay, and there was little sense of cheer. Paul, the logistics master, under pressure from all the groups, worked hard to broker a solution to the depressing logjam. In the event this was to involve a series of helicopter lifts to try to get us all into the mountains. However, due to much tighter payload restrictions this meant that not everyone would be able to get to their original intended destinations. Nevertheless, in the course of two more days, during which a reserve pilot was drafted in, the air movements began, starting with the French who by dint of a little chicanery jumped the queue.

We had to drastically trim our gear and food supplies to meet the strict weight limits, but the prospect of getting inland lightened our hearts. As we squeezed into the helicopter, the pilot handed me a radio headset – "There will be some turbulence, and the weather may yet force a change of plan, so nothing is guaranteed." The rotors of the Jet Ranger flailed the air as the noisy machine fought to climb off the ground in the rain and wind, then slowly picked up speed to push out between the steep flanks of the coastal islands. We caught our breaths as ferocious gusts pushed the helicopter sideways and knuckles whitened when we gripped the seats as unseen downdraughts blasted us closer to the waves in ice-dotted fjords. A rather alarming experience indeed, but at last we were on the way after the long days of inaction.

In contrast to our agitations, the two pilots seemed unconcerned and this was some reassurance against the flying conditions. The throbbing helicopter traced a way northwards above Ammassalik Fjord, passing close to the settlement of Kuummiit then threaded deep valleys to turn over Sermilik Fjord, choked with ice. Veering northeast we flew low over the chaotically fissured and fractured surfaces of the gigantic Midgaard Glacier,

Climbing the Coxcomb Peak summits, Champs-Elysées Glacier

1 The Jet Ranger helicopter leaves us on the Champs-Elysées Glacier 2 A windy day for skiing on the Champs-Elysées Glacier 3 Weather change on 16 September Glacier
4 Climbers on the slopes of Hidden Peak

then moved along the course of the Franche Comté Glacier and on over Femstjernen, a hugely distorted confluence of five major ice flows. After a time we bore eastwards into the jaws of the Champs-Elysées Glacier, the ice dirty with moraine, crossing the Arctic Circle en route, with black rock slopes on both sides sweeping up into fog and low, clinging cloud masking unseen, unclimbed summits.

The pilot's voice crackled into the headset, "This is as far as we can go". He selected a spot on the north edge of the glacier and settled the helicopter onto the ice in a spray of water and motioned us to get out. Hastily we pulled out our kit and threw it down onto the water-runnelled surface. After a quick check for altitude and position co-ordinates, we crouched in the wet blast as the helicopter lifted away to try to make a swift return for our friends still waiting out on the coast at Kulusuk, the engine noise slowly being lost to the sound of wind and the gurgle of water. The wetness of the glacier surface led us to move off along the ice for some distance in search of a better place to camp. In a couple of hours the helicopter was back with our remaining friends. The forced circumstances meant we were now three groups camped slightly apart, but in a day or two intending to head out in different directions so as to have space for independent operation.

Although we had now reached the mountains, the weather was still somewhat unfavourable so we endured another day of immobility before we could ski and pulk our gear eastwards up the Champs-Elysées Glacier to establish a proper base camp in a better setting. The other groups also devised their own plans and the next day we dispersed, each party self-absorbed in its own move. For us this was not without some problems due to crevasses: even on skis we punched some frightening holes through very fragile snowbridges revealing unwelcome views into glacial innards. At last we won out onto more reassuring safer ground with some metres of snow cover and we pressed on along the glacier. Several hours later we stopped in rather gloomy light and pitched tents to make camp in wind and falling snow. For the ten of us there was a night of blizzard and blow, testing us for a while longer. Our Arctic first-timers were more tried by this than those of us who'd already experienced the wonderland of these northern mountains. When the long overdue sun came out, the surrounding peaks were heavily mantled in new snow but it was obvious that rich pickings lay there for the taking if the weather settled. A day of skiing was a more than welcome return to activity and we gained a number of minor summits allowing us to scope the lie of the land and size up other mountains we might try when the risk of avalanche receded somewhat.

The time of our good fortune having arrived, we sought to make the most of our chances, even accepting with some equanimity the night-times of bitter coldness when temperatures fell to minus 24 degrees Celsius. Dividing into two parties we climbed a doubletopped mountain we dubbed the Sphinx, exchanging positions on the head and tail-end summits. The following day produced a very good ascent up the South Ridge of Tangent Peak, its 2,420 metre top formed by a tenuous rock pinnacle with very limited space at its apex. The splendour of the outlook from here soon banished from our minds all the irritations of our recent days of delay.

Across from the camp stood a mountain with a series of prominent rocky towers strung along its crest. Drawn by the prospect of interesting climbing we skied over there the next morning, finding access to the ridge by means of a concealed couloir. By traversing the linking arêtes we could get to the pinnacles, enjoying the exposure. Faced with a deep notch we stared at the final tower before some delicate moves took us up to an impressive prow of rock at the highest point. Feeling very pleased with this success we lingered for a while before seeking a way down avoiding loose rock. Other objectives lay at hand and various partnerships formed to suit preferences. Lying east of the camp, a high peak with a very acute West Ridge appealed to me. I had seen this mountain from afar during my 1994 expedition but it had eluded me then. Now, from close to, it enticed but promised not to be a pushover. Rod, a widely experienced mountaineer offered to team up with me for an attempt. Accordingly, taking advantage of some of the colder hours, we left base at 2:00 am, skiing up to a step at the foot of the ridge.

We worked up through deep snow towards crevasses cutting the crest. The first of these yielded easily to Rod who led on to the second, more of a puzzle in the form of a double fissure. On the left we eventually found a band of hard, solid ice affording safe anchorage on firm ice screws. The upper wall of the bergschrund bulged over a bridge which might allow a traverse towards the corniced edge out on the right. After a fragile start the snowbridge firmed up and I could make exposed progress out to the edge where it was difficult to know how the cornice remained attached to the mountain. Moves up and left led on through very unconsolidated snow where lengthy excavation produced a not totally reassuring belay and stance. Rod followed up and led through and we gained height up the convex ridgeline just left of the cornice with very little in the way of protection until we reached wind-packed snow which offered some degree of security. So it went on, in a finely sculpted position and later we felt comfortable enough to resume moving together, and with huge grins we came along a very acute arête after a satisfying climb. Earlier on we had seen our friends leaving camp for their own chosen peaks and we knew they would have observed us treading our line into the sky. We agreed on naming our mountain the Parrotspitze and our route the Parrot's Beak Arête, in memory of the hooked overhanging serac it had borne three years before. In deference to the snow conditions we decided to seek out a different line for our descent and after traversing for some distance eastwards along the summit ridge we began to climb down a series of ramps on the South Face of the mountain. These led us down into a big couloir where avalanches had swept snow across a large bergschrund. The sun-softened slopes called for a careful progress, and we kept to the couloir edge to try to make use of surer rock anchors. In time we reached the glacier where in rather enervating heat we began to plod the weary kilometres back towards our skis. This was proving to be quite tiring work when unexpectedly one of our friends hove into view. With great generosity he had retrieved our skis and selflessly now delivered them to us, thus in great gratitude we were able to glide back to base with considerable economy of effort.

While the weather held we went on another day over a glacier shelf to the south to reach two mountains we'd noticed from the Parrotspitze, lying in a sidebay. In climbing these two, Hidden Peak and Well-hidden Peak, we enjoyed moving above enormous drops from ridge rims falling away into the Pourquoi-pas Glacier, taking time to sit on summits to gaze at the ranks of mountains ringing the horizons and enjoying the privilege of being out there. At moments like this it felt good to savour the profound silence of our surroundings, underlining our own smallness in these wide tracts of wildness.

Now we were running out of time but still some of the group members found energy to ski away for more climbs. In the last days the other parties converged on our base camp as the rendezvous agreed for pick-up and we enjoyed hearing about their various adventures. Unlike the dispiriting days at the beginning, there were no problems with the ski-plane flights and we were lifted away in batches for a final summit-hopping ride back to the coastal greenery of Kulusuk, feeling that we'd made the most of our period of reprieve and seized our chances when the the time came. A few days of transition at Kulusuk and relaxation back in Iceland rounded out our trip and although we were looking forward to reaching home, there in our minds was the hope for another return to these tempting and rewarding Arctic expanses.

1997 TANGENT EXPEDITION TO THE CHAMPS-ELYSÉES GLACIER, EAST GREENLAND
Paul Walker, Rod Pashley, Phil Lightfoot, Jim Gregson, Jim McLuckie, Peter Baillie, Sandy Gregson, Glenn Morris, Peter Watson and John Starbuck

On the summit ridge of Parrotspitze, a fine first ascent

Skiing out towards virgin peaks in the Kronprins Frederik Bjerge

9   Ski and Pulk

In 1888 the Norwegian Fridtjof Nansen led his pioneering party to make the first crossing of the Greenland icecap. He and his men went on foot or on ski, hauling sledges laden with food and equipment. The precedents that Nansen set were to have an enduring influence on Arctic and Antarctic travellers for a century to come.

Even nowadays, the Nansen-type sledge, a wooden construction held together by lashings which permit a degree of flexibility, is still used by some parties. It is quite different in its nature to the Inuit model, a heavier rigid type pulled traditionally by dog teams and more often now towed behind motorised skidoos. Technological development and newer materials have also produced great advances in the design and construction of skis.

Since the 1980s most groups wishing to travel over the Arctic's icecap areas and glaciers have opted for the use of the more modern pulk for load carrying. In essence this is in the form of a traylike base, moulded in fibreglass for strength, fitted with a fabric cover and provided with a set of alloy towing shafts which connect to a harness worn by the skier. The pulk itself is quite light for its size, usually about two metres long. When loading, the key principle is to try to keep the centre of gravity low, and surprisingly heavy weights can be managed. When snow or ice surfaces are firm and relatively smooth the laden pulk can be fairly easy to pull and once an efficient rhythm is found the whole thing moves ahead quite readily. Rougher surfaces such as pronounced sastrugi, or deeper soft snow lead, as one would expect, to slower rates of progress. For really heavy loads it is also possible to rig up a system for two skiers to pull in tandem, and with co-ordination this method can make for very rapid travel, and certainly has a big advantage for uphill work.

Skiing downhill while towing a pulk puts a greater demand on the skills of the skier. While it is true that the rigid towing bars prevent the pulk from running into the skier from behind, the effects of momentum and gravity can produce a powerful push in the rear which has to be managed. The effects of uneven ground are also transmitted through the harness and towbars so one has to be alert and develop a feel for reading terrain on the move. Turning a heavy pulk must be practised and the radius for changes of direction requires subtle judgement.

For all the idiosyncracies of the pulk, however, its use wins hands down over backpacking under heavy weights, with the proviso that the ground to be negotiated allows the pulk to slide. Thus for forward motion without regression, traction must be sought. I refer here to Nordic-style skiing, where the bindings allow the skier's heels to lift in the classic kick-and-glide action. When no great load is involved, ski traction can be obtained by the application of special waxes to the base of the ski, allowing the snow crystals to grip and prevent any backslipping. For heavier loads or uphill progress, the skis can be fitted with climbing skins. Traditionally these were made from strips of sealskin, but the modern versions consist of synthetic fibre, commonly nylon, with an adhesive backing which sticks onto the base of the ski. When pushed forward the skin and ski slide over the snow: when weighted the ski holds its position. Thus the skier can travel on glacier or icecap, with due care and attention to the possible objective dangers associated with crevasses and avalanche conditions. If the situation calls for skiers to be roped together for safety reasons, then another raft of rescue skills must also be learned and practised.

10 Northern Nights Out

Shackletons Bjerg, Goodenough Land 1998

The Northeast Greenland National Park, largest in the world, is subject to more stringent permit regulations than other parts of the island, so it was intriguing to be invited to join an expedition to these high latitudes. Paul Walker, my companion from earlier trips had put together a fascinating plan for 1998, and offered places on the second phase of his scheme. He'd been away to explore the surroundings of Petermanns Bjerg and as the rest of our group gathered he was staying with his young family in the isolated Scoresbysund village of Ittoqqortoormiit, waiting to join us when we reached the airstrip at Constable Pynt, Nerlerit Inaat, on the shore of Hurry Fjord.

Endearingly, travel arrangements in Greenland are not set in rigid schedules, so we were not too surprised that our transfer from Iceland was re-routed at the last minute and we made a dogleg flight via Kulusuk. Heading northeast from there we overflew hundreds of kilometres of mountain ranges extending through almost ten degrees of latitude, some of them the scenes of our own adventures in previous years, before crossing the still-frozen Scoresbysund and turning over Jameson and Liverpool Lands to come down onto the gravel strip at Constable Pynt.

We passed one rather mosquito-bitten night here so were eager to load up our team kit into the Twin Otter skiplane to fly into the mountains the following morning, crossing en route the southern part of the spectacular Staunings Alps. Further to the northwest the terrain changed to extensive glacier basins with more isolated large mountains as we drew closer to the fringes of the Inland Ice. The few maps we'd obtained were interestingly labelled with tracts of "unexplored territory." After a couple of hours in the air we were landed on a high iceshelf at 2,060 metres, above the snaking course of Nordenskiölds Glacier.

Having got safely into position we used a base camp there for several days to attempt many of the surrounding mountains. But first a new experience. The National Park regulations specified firearm provision against possible polar bear encounters so two .30-06 calibre rifles added weight to our equipment. Once the camp was set up, on the first morning we gathered for a session of target practise, for which purpose a snowman-type figure was built and decked with a cardboard heart. Most of us were able to score some sort of hit on this benign static quarry: fortunately we were not destined to test ourselves against a moving, hungry bear.

The mountains ringing the camp area proved not to be too technically demanding thus serving ideally for honing our fitness levels. The ski approaches were also not so difficult for the neophytes in the party so they were able to fall over without great risk of injury. The ridges on these peaks gave pleasant outings despite the looseness of some of the rock, and from a variety of summits we looked out west onto the Inland Ice. After a few nights, between us we had reached seventeen summits, with everyone gaining some first ascents. Following this period of activity we formulated our future movements. Shackletons Bjerg, away in the east, figured large in our minds due to its dominance, and we broke camp, loading our pulks for a night-time move to a new position closer to its foot. Setting off at 10:00 pm in sunshine, our route led us south then east down a side glacier losing about 300 metres of height to arrive at the edge of the huge Nordenskiölds Glacier, moraine-striped and broken by many crevasses.

Nearing the summit of Shackletons Bjerg

1

2

3

4

1 Sandy Gregson on Link Peak, the central summit of Orion's Belt Traverse   2 Tangent group climbers on Orion's Belt Traverse to Snow Queen   3 Tundra landing by Twin Otter at Kjerulfs Fjord
4 Shackletons Bjerg seen from Pulk Peak

Beyond the glacier, superbly lit by the low-angled sun, rose the full height of the West Face of Shackletons Bjerg, a splendid insular pyramid waiting to be climbed. But first the glacier crossing had to be tackled.

The very broken surface was also complicated by substantial areas of meltwater which, although skinned with thin ice in the early hours, we'd have to avoid. As we were skiing roped up in small teams, coping with the heavy pulk-loads made for slow going. For more than four kilometres we zigzagged back and forth among the crevasses, following the line carefully and expertly probed by Nigel out at the front of our column until a re-ascent on another side glacier permitted us to gain a suitable location for our second camp at about 1,840 metres. This moving had taken almost ten hours of fairly heavy slog so we were glad to re-pitch tents and sleep, until the daytime heat drove us from our sleeping bags.

After the exertions needed to shift camp, most people wanted to have an easier night but Sandy and I were tempted by the summit of Shackletons Bjerg glinting away a thousand metres above. In the late evening we pushed our skis on skins up to a shoulder by the toe of the South West Ridge where we switched into climbing boots and crampons. We were blessed with flat calm air and cheering sunshine as we gained height over steep rises and bumps which concealed then revealed the mountain's upper slopes. The beautiful raking light from the sun delayed us into bouts of photography but as it was actually midnight there was no fear of running out of time. We marvelled at the immense triangle of shadow which this large mountain cast far out for many kilometres to the south enveloping neighbouring glaciers and peaks in cold blue shade.

Closer to the top, the ridge fined down into a series of narrow ice arêtes running above the steep West Face. For some time the summit was capped by a bonnet of convected mist suffused with a golden glow, which faded as the vapour dissipated. We enjoyed traversing these more exposed sections and soon after we drew up to the culminating point. The stillness and clarity of the night air allowed us to absorb the spacious panorama in an unhurried way. In the north stood the pyramidal bulk of Petermanns Bjerg, the major peak of the High Arctic: eastwards were the serrations of the Staunings Alps: to south and west immense icecap zones, and over in the northwest the many nunataks fringing the Inland Ice, among them those we had ascended during the previous week. Abruptly below us was the perforated and stone-striped stream of Nordenskiölds Glacier, serpentining along its deep trench to debouch into distant Kejser Franz Josephs Fjord. Sandy and I relished our climb to this summit, first reached in 1953, savouring the fact of being just two on such a fine mountain, although observed, we later learned, by our friends who at the same time had climbed to the top of a lower peak across the glacier to the south. We climbed down happily to our skis and made a speedy run down to camp over the frozen surface. The next night we traded places, Sandy coming with me to make a ski ascent of Pulk Peak from which we watched our friends repeat the climb of Shackletons Bjerg in perfect conditions to give a full group success.

In the course of the next evening, six of the team struck camp and skied away southeast to find a fresh position at the head of the Passage Glacier. Meanwhile with Sandy I pushed up the glacier passing Shackletons Bjerg for a few kilometres, until we were leaving our skis in a deep meltwater hollow ringed by broken crags at the foot of a satellite peak. A climb along an arête of rock then ice brought us up to its summit at 2,530 metres. Back at the skis we noticed how our voices reverberated round the hollow so our mountain became Echo Pond Peak. During the next afternoon the remaining eight of us packed up our camp then followed the ski tracks left by our team-mates for fifteen kilometres to the place where they'd sited a new and final camp overlooking the Passage Glacier.

This was handily placed for access to a number of appealing peaks, and through the next few nights we garnered a further twenty summits. Only a short distance away lay the three mountains which became Orion's Belt, so dubbed by Keith and Andrea, joining the summits of Nevis, Link Peak and Snow Queen. Climbing them gave a superb traverse on high ridges and we all enjoyed the outing in various combinations over the next three nights, with some variation starts by steeper couloirs on the North Face of Nevis. Numerous additional forays were completed, with people climbing as they fancied from the ample choice to hand. For Sandy and me, a good excursion was secured by making a long tra verse taking in the five prominent rocky Molars punctuating the Toothed Ridge, before crossing to the higher summit of Mørkefinger.

As our time dwindled away we had to consider our eventual exit from the mountains. Originally, Paul had proposed that some of us should try to descend on foot along the Passage Glacier then continue all the way to the coast for a pick-up at sea level. This idea had arisen because we knew that the skiplane was unavailable to us at the required time for other contractual reasons, although we could get a wheeled aircraft but obviously not to and from a glacier. A helicopter would be needed to lift equipment to a suitable landing area which had been identified in advance. However, while Sandy and I had been on the top of Mørkefinger we had been able to see down onto and along the Passage Glacier and its continuation river course through deeply cut Agassiz Dal which was our proposed exit route. This fortuitous reconnaissance showed us a fractured glacier falling into a string of gorges where the outflow river plunged over numerous waterfalls and looked extremely unlikely as a feasible way for us to attempt to reach the coast.

When this intelligence was relayed to the prospective overland party the idea of a pedestrian exit lost its exploratory appeal somewhat. As we had the helicopter arrangement in any case, it proved possible to negotiate an extension of flying time so that everyone could be flown down to the shoreline. We had now been joined by a second group, the personnel of Derby Mountain Rescue Team, who had been active in the mountains east of Shackletons Bjerg, and were sharing, for reasons of cost, in our flight arrangements. The Derby men had thoughtfully provisioned themselves with ample supplies of "disinfectant" for their trip and in order to avoid taking it back home unused, we joined them for a final evening in their mess tent where these supplies cheerfully transmogrified into a variety of malt whiskies which were duly sampled and enjoyed by those of us partial to such delightful tastes.

Early on the next morning we had all the kit packed and assembled when the smallish helicopter buzzed into view over the rim of the Passage Glacier icefall. The pilot was most co-operative and we arranged a mix of sling-loads and people flights to transfer down to the head of Kjerulfs Fjord. Flying down confirmed to us the probably impenetrable nature of the gorges in Agassiz Dal and we were relieved not to be trying to force a way through the waterfall-decked defiles. As we approached the tundra slopes by the head of Kjerulfs Fjord the pilot pointed out to us the dust clouds kicked up by the hooves of groups of Musk Oxen scattering before the helicopter roar as we descended. The sharp contrast from glacier ice and mountains to vegetated fjord shore and running water was very marked as we stepped out of the helicopter to see icebergs grounded in tidewater. A few days camped there would have been a pleasant coda, but we had little time to contemplate it. During one of the flights while carrying a loaded net slung beneath the helicopter a pair of skis escaped its lashing and fell to the Passage Glacier. By good fortune the keen-eyed pilot had noticed this fugitive kit and noted its position. In the course of a subsequent flight he held the helicopter in a daring hover only just off the ice then persuaded a very intrepid climber to jump out onto the glacier to retrieve the skis and hand them up before scrambling back aboard himself to allow the flight to resume.

A very short time after our arrival at Kjerulfs Fjord, while we were admiring flowers in amongst the mosses, a new engine noise came to our ears as a Twin Otter droned into sight, circling quickly, then came in to make a spectacular and bumpy landing on the rough tundra surface. Within minutes we had our belongings on board and were soon airborne again, impressed by the skills of the pilots coping with the demands of take-off from unprepared ground, leaving the dust to settle behind us as we banked to head out along the lengths of Dicksons, Kempes and later Kong Oscars Fjords, passing the northern edges of the Staunings Alps. The aeroplane then turned to run in towards the airstrip at Mestersvig, formerly serving a very active leadmining site close by. From there we would shortly begin our return journey to Iceland to close another sojourn into Greenland's mountain treasure chest. At Reykjavík we had a few awkward minutes explaining why we were reclaiming a large rifle from the baggage claim area: it had been loaded onto the plane inadvertently during the rush to get away. The customs officer was not amused and we were glad that he decided to confiscate it while we were more interested in taking a shower and heading for a bar.

1998 TANGENT EXPEDITION TO SHACKLETONS BJERG, NORTHEAST GREENLAND
Paul Walker, Steve Ripley, Alan Law, Nigel Edwards, Keith Partridge, John Burton, Nicky Edwards, Andrea Partridge, Diane Burton, Jim Gregson, Steph McDearmid, David Jehan, Sandy Gregson and Matt Sutcliffe

North from Echo Pond Peak to the pyramid shape of Petermanns Bjerg – time 1:00 am

A difficult deep-snow landing for the Twin Otter

A helicopter departs
from Tasiilaq Fjeldhytte

Relaxing in camp below Shackletons Bjerg

11   Tent Time

Almost every television or cinema film set in the Arctic or Antarctic, documentary or fiction, seems to come with a soundtrack of howling wind and blowing spindrift. It would be foolish, of course, to claim that this never happens but in my own experience the conditions associated with prolonged exposure to powerful sunshine are more frequent.

For some, the prospect of camping for extended periods of time on glacier or icecap may cause an involuntary shiver. There can be, for sure, times when conditions are something of a trial but experience teaches the requisite methods of successful coping. Modern equipment helps too, but as in any undertaking there are "tricks of the trade."

The best tents for the Arctic are the multi-pole geodesic or semigeodesic types. These are self-supporting and provide the best balance of size and usable space. Once securely staked down they can cope with very strong winds, flexing then resuming their normal shape. Even without sufficient snowstakes, guylines can be strongly anchored by being attached to a bag filled with snow which is then stamped in and buried where it quickly freezes solidly into place. Inside the tent goes a wall-to-wall sheet of thin closed-cell foam, and over that one's individual thicker foam sleep mat plus a self-inflating mattress. All this provides insulation from the underlying cold surface of the snow and reduces the chance of condensation forming on the tent floor. A good-quality down-filled sleeping bag then provides the immediate warmth for restorative sleep.

Some of my friends like to build protective walls from snow blocks to deflect wind from their tents. My own preference is usually not to do this from the outset, letting the wind blow any loose material away. If staying in the same location for some time, the wind eventually begins to deposit snow in the lee of the tents and after storm it becomes necessary to shovel drift away. Thus one ends up with a wall in any case. It is, though, worth experimenting with the construction of smaller wind deflector structures at a short distance upwind of tents, as they can be modelled to redirect spindrift away from a camp and minimise the need for digging out.

Expedition groups must bring with them almost all of their requirements in terms of food and fuel supply for cooking. This latter requires some careful advance calculation, for in glaciated regions water must often be obtained by melting snow or ice. Here the sun becomes an ally. By rigging up a black bag, polythene or other material, hanging above a suitable container, solar radiation can be relied on to produce a steady drip of meltwater which saves on fuel usage.

The sun can cause other problems though. In the Arctic summer there is twenty four hour daylight and without wind the sun's strength is very obvious. It is common, if not customary, to be active in the nominal night-time hours for skiing and climbing purposes, with sleep and rest occurring in the middle of the day. At times this can be a great deal warmer than one might expect so it can be useful to have some sort of sheeting to drape over a tent roof to create a cooler, more comfortable zone of shade on the inside. A tent used for several expeditions may in time suffer from deterioration in the fabric due to the effects of exposure to ultra-violet light. This causes even strong synthetics like nylon to fade in colour and become brittle and prone to tearing. Seeing this serves as a very firm reminder of the importance of using good sunscreen creams on exposed areas of one's own skin.

A well-organised camp, with careful stowage of equipment is worth the trouble. In its environs, much of the social interaction of an expedition is conducted, plans are laid and success is celebrated. The camp is also one's refuge in adverse weather, a retreat from storm and the hub of activity.

For some like myself, there is a certain sense of nostalgia for the more complete feeling of isolation and remoteness of my earliest Arctic venturings. In more recent times the advent of more reliable satellite telecoms and the use of GPS has reduced the perception of being cut off to some extent, but one only has to endure a protracted Arctic storm to realise that in these northerly locations the weather still holds the most powerful hand and even in dire time of emergency one is at the mercy of the elements.

Base camp on the Woolley Glacier, Watkins Bjerge

12   On the Roof of the Arctic

Watkins Bjerge – Gunnbjørns Fjeld 1999

Maternal Eider Ducks with their crèches of downy ducklings waddled unconcernedly along and across the runway at Isafjorður airport in northwest Iceland, for the most part oblivious to aircraft landing and taking off. We were waiting for our onward charter flight to take us over the Denmark Strait and into the Watkins Bjerge, Greenland's highest range of peaks, capped by Gunnbjørns Fjeld, at 3,693 metres the roof of the Arctic.

These mountains were discovered from the air on 1 September 1930 by Gino Watkins and Flt-Lt N H D'Aeth during a survey flight as part of the British Arctic Air Route Expedition. Even from a distance of 100 kilometres (ca. 70 miles) they established that these were the highest of the Arctic's mountains, but difficulties of access were to protect them from bootprints for some time. Watkins himself never had the chance to climb in this region and the mountains only bear his name as a posthumous honour conferred by the government of Denmark, ironic in the light of Watkins's stated preference for the use of local nomenclature where possible. During Martin Lindsay's 1934 British Trans-Greenland Expedition, which crossed the icecap from west to east then continued southwest on the fringe of the Inland Ice to Ammassalik, the position of "The Monarch," Lindsay's name for the tallest peak was fixed by ground survey with considerable accuracy. After further aerial surveys it was officially renamed as Gunnbjørns Fjeld. The account of its first ascent written by Jack Longland who was a member of the first ascent party from Lawrence Wager's 1935 expedition makes interesting reading with its description of the lengthy approach by a party on skis hauling sledges after a difficult landing at the complex fjord coast.

By the curious logic of twenty four hour daylight and private charters we were able to study a variety of birdlife on a series of pools and lagoons just off the airport tarmac – Redthroated Divers, Redshanks, a bunch of Rednecked Phalaropes and a whole colony of garrulous yet graceful Arctic Terns – until our turn to fly came just after midnight. The five of us boarded the small Twin Otter skiplane and took off into the non-setting sun in the middle of June. After only thirty minutes of flying out over the ocean we crossed the edge of the pack ice stretching out this year a long, long way from the Greenland coast and not yet starting its summer breakup. Later on the darker shapes of the mountains climbed above the horizon and then we were among them, threading a way towards the big glacier on which we were to land.

The pilot turned the aircraft between striking white peaks and we slanted down to a smooth touchdown on the even surface at 3:30 am in bright sunshine. We stepped out into fairly deep snow then quickly pulled all of our gear and rucksacks from the plane to allow the crew to get away home to Iceland. Once the little machine was gone, blasting us with blown snow as it went, cold silence gripped the scene and we hurried to get our tents pitched and the kettle on. Here at 2,560 metres near the head of the Woolley Glacier, we were in a location where fewer than five previous groups had ever been, and we were interested in some of the unclimbed mountains which surrounded us. As we made our camp, the sun travelled along a low arc across the northern sky, reminding us that there would be no darkness during our stay amid these impressive peaks.

Skiing up towards Gunnbjørns Fjeld, the peak on the left

The descent line from Terra Nova Peak *Photo: Scott Umpleby*

Later in the morning, the sun's strength made it feel too warm to stay in sleeping bags and we emerged from the tents to orientate ourselves.

Not so far away were some very good looking peaks as well as some of the bigger mountains which number among the highest in Greenland. After we'd sorted our kit we agreed between the five of us that we would try to get up some of the virgin tops, choosing from the more elegant ones as well as trying to reach some of the higher summits. Gordon, at 64 our oldest team member, was keen to find some mountains suitable for ski ascents, protesting his nontechnical climber status: in the event he coped splendidly with everything we tried and surpassed his own expectations. The next day brought mist and light snowfall but we left the tents to ski out to the Bear's Claw group of peaks which stood round the head of the glacier in the east. Having reached the base of our chosen mountain we kicked steps up the narrowing North Ridge of Forefinger, 3,367 metres, the so far unclimbed tenth-highest peak in Greenland, straining to see how close we were to the corniced edge. At the top we waited in gentle snowfall for a clearance which never came thus robbing us of any view, before we descended to ski back to camp happy with a first ascent but regretting not having had a wider outlook.

In the following day we decided to try to get onto a night-time schedule for climbing to benefit from firmer surfaces and safer conditions, and set out in the evening heading northwards to some more untouched peaks. Again we were overtaken by mist and poor visibility as we climbed up a steepening ridge. It was difficult to decipher the precise edge except where a couple of rock steps barred progress as we balanced up over rather loose blocks. We came out onto a first one, then a second, snow summit – Terra Nova Peak, 3,020 metres. The mist began to disperse and we emerged into sunshine, reminding ourselves that it came from low down on the horizon to our north as it was the middle of the night. We were hoping to traverse our peak and continue on to its neighbour, but the ground fell away very steeply down a convex slope into dead ground out of our sight. Scott offered to go down on a rope to investigate, so I stamped out a big bucket seat in the snow from which to anchor him. He was soon back to say that two ropelengths would allow us to gain a narrow linking arête, so I stayed in my ice-upholstered seat to safeguard everyone down. Scott re-descended

Lichen Bjerg from the South West Ridge of Gunnbjørns Fjeld

Gunnbjørns Fjeld, highest summit in Greenland, pierces the clouds

to a double deadman anchor, then the others followed, and eventually I could lever myself out of my cold stance and go down to the exposed perch where the others had stopped. Without delay we crossed to the narrow arête and set off in a fine position to go up to the top of Flash Point, 2,960 metres, another peak unclimbed before now. The improving light and dissipating mists revealed to us more of the encircling landscape highlighted by beautiful raking sunbeams and we had our first sighting across the glaciers to Gunnbjørns Fjeld itself, standing clear above its satellite peaks.

After a pleasant, unhurried spell of reconnaissance time we made our way down another ridge, completing a horseshoe traverse to recover our skis before travelling back to camp. Subsequent to these successes we thought we might go a little higher so for a next outing we tried to make a ski ascent of Julia, 3,455 metres, and Greenland's seventh-highest point. This went well at first, as we skinned up the mountain's eastern flanks until we approached 3,200 metres, but we realised that the weather was working towards a change. The sky clouded up and very quickly strong winds began to gust and blast us with spindrift. As this became more uncomfortable we renounced our climb and turned downhill. Getting off was made difficult by the now fierce wind unbalancing us on our skis, and we were glad to regain the shelter of our camp. Unfortunately this proved to be the onset of a three-day on and off storm which kept us tentbound apart from spells outside to shovel off the encroaching drifts.

When the weather began to settle again we were wary about the potential avalanche conditions so we agreed on making an attempt to ski to the top of Paul-Emile Victor, the fourth-ranking of Greenland's peaks at 3,609 metres, and one of Gordon's favoured objectives. This gave us a very long day out as even on skis we were sinking into copious fresh snow, but by winding up glacial bays avoiding obvious crevasses we found ourselves after some hours skinning up the final gentle slopes to a flattish summit area. Around us stretched countless peaks, mostly unclimbed, and over in the northwest the obvious summit block of Gunnbjørns Fjeld seemed to float above a sea of cloud, its crowning height emphatic over all its rivals. We had a great return, with splendid ski running on deep powder snow in the sunlit areas and crisper going where our line took us through shade and we felt good to be active after the storm days.

Although keen to measure ourselves against Gunnbjørns Fjeld now we'd seen it from afar, we were strongly drawn by one more peak just north of our camp, from which dropped a very sharply defined arête. Reverting to the night-time routine we soon skied over to its foot, and made a very direct ascent on the honed crest to capture the summit of Midnight Peak, 3,249 metres. Despite the sunshine sparkling off the snow it was very cold at this top: Scott, Gordon and Jon chose not to linger and reversed the route of ascent, while Sandy and I pushed on to find a way off via the East Ridge, descending steeply to make a full traverse of the mountain. We worked down into a col below a striking adjacent peak where we encountered very deep and very cold powder snow deposited here during the recent storm. After some tiring wading we exited into a glacier combe to rejoin our friends and our skis.

As we had arranged for our skiplane to collect us from close to Gunnbjørns Fjeld we now made a decision to move our camp, so we loaded and harnessed up our pulks to make this move. Again travelling in the colder evening hours, we set off along the easy gradients of the wide Woolley Glacier using peaks in Knud Rasmussen Land to the north as steering guides. Swinging round a ridge-end we carefully negotiated a complex crevasse zone then turned to reascend by a tributary glacier to reach a suitable camping area from where we might attempt Gunnbjørns Fjeld. With a few short stops, a ten-hour effort was needed to complete this move, covering over twenty five kilometres. The next day was voted for rest and recovery, although we did spend a couple of hours practising telemark turns to earn our dinners.

Gunnbjørns Fjeld is quite a handsome mountain to behold and we felt that we might reach it without an interim camp if we skied as high as possible. Accordingly, as the chosen day cooled, we left our camp at 7:00 in evening light to begin working our way up the long glacier slopes which would lead us to the mountain's South West Ridge. Steeper sections and some prominent crevasses punctuated our zigzagging line of advance, and we gradually gained height until we felt that skiing was no longer feasible. Here, at 3,300 metres, we switched to crampons and roped into two teams to step up onto the crest of the South West Ridge. The ground steepened where we had to pass some short rock outcroppings,

Reaching Midnight Peak – first ascent by the obvious arête

Descent from a near miss on Dome, Qaqqaq Johnson

from where the defined ridge gave out onto the final slopes. With wide grins we arrived at the summit at four o'clock in the morning, excited to be here on Greenland's highest spot, congratulating each other. The air was calm and we were in sunshine so we could relish our position. Gordon beamed with delight to be here, and for Scott and Jon on their first Arctic trips this was rather special. For Sandy and myself, this region provided interesting contrasts to the other parts of Greenland we'd visited. To the west, beyond the immense Christian IVs Glacier, the Lemon Mountains and the Lindbergh Fjelde ranges rolled out: in the north the glittering icecap and the dark peaks of Knud Rasmussens Land: to the east the rest of the Watkins Bjerge and the bulk of Ejnar Mikkelsens Fjeld, backed by mountains for which scarcely any map exists – great reservoirs of possibility for the adventurous future traveller. When we had photographed and stared to our heart's content we retraced our steps down to the skis. From there we launched off on ten kilometres of magical ski running on firm surfaces, putting in hundreds of turns as we lost height, finally sliding back into camp after a thirteen-hour round trip, well satisfied but hungry.

In the final days of the expedition we went out again to try to climb the second and third highest summits of Qaqqaq Johnson and Qaqqaq Kershaw – formerly known more prosaically as Dome and Cone – approaching on skis up a branch glacier. On Johnson we climbed over a forepeak to get to the long North East Ridge where we progressed to a height of 3,600 metres until we encountered very dubious windslab slopes which fractured ominously round our feet. Judgement overruled ambition and although the summit was very close we turned our steps away and came down carefully to content ourselves with another very long ski descent. We could only be mildly disappointed for we'd had great fun on our first ascents and we'd been to the top of Gunnbjørns Fjeld. Our days in these wonderful mountains had enriched our lives and we'd be going home happy.

The waiting time for the aeroplane extended through a whole day longer than we anticipated. We couldn't confirm the date directly as by one of those oddly satisfying failures of technology our satellite phone had let us down on the back of dud batteries which despite many hours of solar charging delivered no power. We sat and conversed, we brewed

Clearing weather in the Watkins Bjerge

The Twin Otter arrives in the Watkins Bjerge to close another expedition

tea and drank, we watched and listened to rockfall from the closest mountains, we readjusted to not being fully in control. We existed.

The weather held and after another chilly night where we squeezed into one tent we listened for the sound of engine noise. When it came there was the usual bustle to gather the few remaining items together for loading. Once we were on board the aeroplane, I timed the interval between full power and lift-off at just 15 seconds with the Twin Otter charging itself into the air then turning in some turbulence to narrowly clear the mountain tops as we headed east towards the cold blue and white of the ice-marked sea.

1999 TANGENT EXPEDITION TO GUNNBJØRNS FJELD AND THE WATKINS BJERGE
Scott Umpleby, Dr Jon Dallimore, Gordon Downs, Jim Gregson and Sandy Gregson

Kap Dan village, Kulusuk, typical of East Greenland settlements

13   A Welcome for Strangers

The weather had been kind to us for almost two weeks, but as we loaded our equipment onto pulks and into rucksacks the sky began to show the first signs of a deterioration. The descent of the long glacier towards the coast went a little slower than I'd have liked for my companions seemed to lack confidence in their skiing skills. The tongue of the glacier fell away in a steep convexity, fortunately without crevasses. I found a way off it to one side, in a sideslipping traverse leading into an ablation valley flanked by moraine slopes. John, following behind, but not very familiar with towing a pulk, misjudged his line for the traverse and the weight of his load trying to slip downhill eventually flipped him into a fall. Luckily he was not injured apart from bruised dignity. Once we were all off the glacier we faced a few kilometres down a shallow valley to reach the shoreline and the frozen surface of the sea. When we moved onto the sea ice I urged the others to try to step up the pace. We were heading out to the village of Kuummiut from where we would later take a helicopter flight to Tasiilaq.

The pack ice areas, in winter and spring, are the normal habitat for Polar Bears, as their usual prey, the seals, also occupy this zone. For reasons of weight-saving, on this trip we did not take a rifle, so I had been hoping that we could avoid having to make a camp along the shore. Our rather slow rate of progress and the worsening weather prevented us from completing the distance to the settlement in one day. Along the tideline the sea ice was cracked and jumbled into ridges. In places the surface was darkened with kelp, the seaweed frozen into the ice then torn free as the rise and fall of the tides overturned the blocks. Late in the day in the face of powerful winds we made the decision to stop and pitch tents.

For the camp we went up onto an elevated knoll on the shore, the better, we thought, to be able to see the approach of any marauding bear. The next thirty hours proved to be a trying period of storm. The wind increased in strength, shrieking between the steep mountain slopes on either flank of the sound where we were. Snowfall, sleet and rain took their turns to lash the tents. We tried to sleep and when this was not possible we fretted for the security of our shelter. Any bears in our proximity were also sensibly not out and about. Pressure of time saw us striking our camp after the second night of discomfort. We wrestled with the tents to get everything stowed for travel. This turned into hard pulling as by now the snow cover on top of the sea ice was turning into slush. We were getting wet and with leather ski boots now leaking I worried in silence for our feet.

After a few hours I was relieved to see at last the first clear evidence that we were closing on Kuummiut, a disused cabin. We left the sea ice and struggled up onto the shore then up a long gradient to the outskirts of the village. I had the name of one of the local residents with whom we hoped to make contact, but no idea of where his home was located. As we slowly passed more of the wooden houses typical of East Greenland settlements, I began to notice a number of villagers on foot. Several of them carried flowers, but none wanted to stop to speak: later we were told that the funeral of a prominent local was in progress. After a short distance further a woman at a doorway responded to my questioning. "Karl Christian Bajaares hus?" I asked. A moment of incomprehension, then a raised arm and a pointed finger, indicating up yet another slope to where more houses clustered.

Leaving the others, I went on foot until I was among the buildings. By chance a group of school-age children appeared. "Karl Christian Bajaares hus?" I asked again. The girls pointed to one of the houses with steps up to the door and weather-beaten paintwork. A large group of sledgedogs were tethered at random in the wet and stained snow in front of the building. At first my knockings at the door drew no reply, but then a curtain twitched at a nearby window revealing the face of a very small child. The door then opened and a young man of perhaps twenty years of age was giving me a puzzled look. "Karl Christian Bajaare?" He shook his head, but fortune smiled: he understood a little English. "Karl Christian is my father, but he is not here. He's at Grandma's. I can take you there."

The young fellow turned to fetch a coat and boots and strode off further into the village while I followed. At the right house he went inside and soon after, an older man came to the door smiling broadly. This was Karl Christian. He knew one of my close friends from a previous visit when he had arranged a cabin for accommodation and taken him on a dogsledging excursion. Karl Christian spoke good English, so I was quickly able to explain things to him. I had a group of three others, we were all wet, we needed a place to stay for one night before our helicopter flight due the next day. He told me to bring my companions up to his house where he would meet us. When I got back to the others they were relieved to learn

that we would not need to sleep again in our sodden tents. At the house, Karl Christian insisted that everything we had must be carried inside. With his son helping we manhandled skis, rucksacks and even pulks past the dogs and through the doorway and on into the kitchen, well-heated by an oil burning stove. I felt rather embarrassed as water from our kit pooled on the floor. "Don't worry. It will all dry out in time. Come inside and sit down, and let's have some coffee."

After we'd begun to explain about where we'd been and come from, Karl Christian told us that just now he didn't have a cabin with space but we could spend the night here in his own home if we were prepared to sleep on the floor. As the room was thickly carpeted we did not see this as any hardship, and we felt we would offend if we quibbled. The coffee was good, and our host was astounding us with his hospitality. His command of English came as a result of time spent as a ship's cook in the merchant marine trade when he had travelled widely. Now, back in his homeland he worked as a licensed outfitter. He related how he provided dogsledging trips in the winter and spring, and in the summer months from a boat he owned he catered for fishermen after catches as large as the Greenland shark.

He would help us to confirm the times for our helicopter flight, and insisted that we would eat a meal with him and his wife that same evening, although she did not yet know this. When we'd been in the house for

more than an hour, Karl Christian's wife returned home from her job as a teacher in the village school. If she bridled to find her home full with four strangers, and her kitchen strewn with dripping wet belongings, she did not reveal it to us. Although she spoke hardly any English, she too made us feel most welcome.

Dry and warm again, we passed a very pleasant evening in the comfort of this Inuit home. After a hearty meal we were even shown the traditional costumes worn by Inuit women and girls on special occasions and feastdays. This was quite a contrast to the impressively sized television set positioned on one side of the room, on which Karl Christian's younger children and some of their visiting friends watched satellite channel programmes. Although we insisted on making payment for our stay in the house, Karl Christian protested that we were proffering too much but we pressed him to accept.

As we left the next morning to go to the helipad, I couldn't help thinking about what sort of reception a group of foreign strangers might get if they knocked at a door in a small English village in a rainstorm late on a winter's day.

Niviarsiaq – the Maiden, Greenland's national flower

14 Nocturnes

Climbs in the Rignys Bjerg Ranges 2001

Before 1998 nobody had investigated or explored the mountains and glaciers of the Rignys Bjerg area of northeast Greenland. This is a huge expanse of country stretching through latitudes 69 and 70 degrees North, all the way from the Sortebræ ranges to Kap Brewster at the mouth of Scoresbysund – Kangertittivaq – paralleling the Blosseville Coast.

In each year from 1998 through to 2000, a couple of British groups began to visit to explore and climb and open up the region, although there was still no clear evidence that a specific "Rignys Bjerg" itself actually could be identified. My own chance to travel into these mountains came in 2001 when I led a group there for Tangent Expeditions International. I had five companions for the trip: Norman Vernon, Rob MacCallum, Graham Poole, Dave Rothery and again my wife, Sandy. We'd flown out to Iceland: actually we'd flown out to Iceland twice in the same day for on the first occasion there had been a couple of scary aborted landing attempts at Keflavík in thick fog before the airline in its wisdom advised the pilot that he must divert. Annoyingly this diversion was made all the way back to Glasgow! Once properly in Iceland we transferred to Isafjorður to wait for our skiplane to show up. We spent a night at the so-called Summer Hotel which describes the eminently sensible use of the accommodation facilities at the local boarding school outside of termtime, and also spent an hour or two amongst the fascinating miscellany of artefacts at the town museum.

We were having to wait because the aeroplane, on charter from Air Iceland, was busy shuttling other groups into various locations before it was due to collect us. A phone call from the company's charter sales manager warned us of some poor weather over in the Rignys Bjerg area

and a delay because of an unspecified "technical problem" with the aircraft. Resigned to a second night in Isafjorður we were just heading off to a downtown cafe when I was surprised to get another call only twenty minutes later asking me to get the group over to the airport. Air Iceland was going to send its second Twin Otter to fly us unexpectedly to Constable Pynt just north of Scoresbysund. When this aeroplane arrived on wheeled-only undercarriage, it carried not only our eqipment, previously freighted out to Akureyri, but also a mechanic, a huge jack and a complete aircraft wheel. Still slightly puzzled by this extra cargo, we looked down onto the dense pack ice in the Denmark Strait, thinking about the recently discovered wreck of HMS Hood, sunk in these waters in 1941 while pursuing the German battleship Bismarck.

The little plane crossed the coast of Greenland and turned northeast to wing down in sunlight towards Constable Pynt. As we made the final approach it became obvious that the runway was obstructed, for there in the middle of the levelled gravel we could see the red-painted wing of the first Twin Otter which was listing markedly to port. Our landing had to be abrupt and short, and after we'd disembarked the airport manager asked us to keep out of the way while work began immediately to repair the plane's landing gear. On returning from a flight to the Watkins Bjerge for refuelling, the ski-equipped Twin Otter had suffered a major tyre blowout and a badly mangled wheel on landing. Luckily the thing hadn't flipped over.

Two hours elapsed before we were summoned to board the repaired aircraft: the mechanic had clearly earned his overtime pay. We were soon in the air again en route now for our planned destination. We passed over

Rignys Bjerg, 2,680m, seen from South Side Traverse

Climbers on South Side Traverse

the filigree patterns of ice in the still fast frozen Scoresbysund then headed southwest for an hour peering down on increasingly impressive mountains and intensely bluepooled and moraine-banded glaciers. Soon there was a straight-in descent and touchdown on the ice of the Broadway Glacier. Here for a rendezvous and pickup were the members of the Royal Navy Arctic Explorer Expedition led by Brian Pancott. They had made a number of ascents on the borders of the icecap in the previous two or three weeks. Their original landing had been at a much greater elevation on the icecap but the pilots had requested a lower pick-up point because of summer snowmelt so they had moved down to our intended base location. For a team which preferred snowshoes to skis they had covered a lot of ground.

After twenty five minutes the sailors and the Twin Otter were off and we were left in the always impressive silence of "the Big White." For the newcomers to the Arctic, tent-pitching was punctuated by stop and stare moments, and happy grins greeted the roar of stoves as we made hot drinks. In the early hours of the morning, lit by soft sunlight from the north, we settled in for some sleep. Later in the day we had the camp shipshape and the kit sorted and were in discussions about our potential outings. An exploratory ski tour was agreed on, to help loosen our legs, orientate ourselves in relation to our aerial photographs, and identify peaks and routes we might attempt.

Although Greenland glaciers often permit unroped skiing, we wore harnesses and took crevasse rescue gear and rope for this tour. All of us were competent or good skiers which made for easy movement as we headed off along the West Side Glacier, studying south faces of mountains to our right and north faces to our left. Stopping periodically to locate peaks on our aerial photo-map, we aimed ourselves towards a very prominent rock pyramid of a mountain and turned up into a glacier bay to go up to a col in a bounding ridge to gain a vantage point. Across the glacier behind us rose an attractive arête to a high white peak which we noted as a worthwhile objective for later in the trip. Progressing more steeply up towards the col, Norman had difficulty getting his non-waxing skis to grip and took them off to walk. Just before breasting the col we encountered a little cluster of crevasses. I paused here to warn Norman to

be watchful, then joined Rob, Dave and Sandy who by then had crossed over and disappeared behind some rocks to shelter from a cool breeze. A few minutes later there was some urgent yelling from below. We looked around the rocks to see only Norman's head and arms above the snow, and Graham looking on anxiously a short way behind. A snowbridge had broken as Norman had stepped onto it, but with very quick reactions he had dived forward to jam his ski poles into the upper lip of the crevasse and stopped with his body and legs swinging free in the cavity. Galvanized by this sight we got a rope to him with great haste and pulled him to safety, then belayed Graham across to safe ground too.

After this excitement and a drinks stop were over, we continued our tour passing beneath the north side of the pyramid, Norman being understandably a touch subdued. Although imposing from a distance the mountain seemed to consist of layers of very rotten rock so we left it off our list of things to try. Now we looked for a descent back to the West Side Glacier further to the west and were a little disappointed that where our photographs suggested plain sailing we found a convex sweep of slope with several seracs. After some zigzagging we forced a way down via a long diagonal traverse with some sidestepping and a lot of sideslipping. However we'd seen several other goodlooking mountains which would be accessible from our camp and after covering a good distance we glided back to base and tried to sleep in the daylight hours. This was difficult due to the heat from the sun, and for much of the time our sleeping bags were more useful as shades over our tents rather than as bedding.

Just how powerful the sunshine was became clear the next night when we attempted the South Face of a peak merely one hour's skiing out of camp. Climbing in two ropes of three, we postholed our way up steep snow until at two-thirds height we gathered on a rock island and decided that conditions were not safe enough to continue. After a watchful retreat we concluded that future route choices should be confined to north-facing slopes or ridges which enjoyed some prolonged shade during the sun's twenty four hour round. We set out on a second ski tour the next night, heading southwest into Hole-in-the-Wall Glacier where we saw more attractive mountains that might go onto our list. Crossing back over Broadway we approached Outlook Col. From there we could see right along the enormous glacier system of Sortebrae, flanked by masses of untouched mountains, and to the south the highest parts of the Rignys Bjerg district, too far away for us to realistically get to we decided. Time for some more climbing. Easy skiing across Broadway to the south put us below the elegant snow and ice arête of Whiteliner Peak which we climbed as a start to the South Side Traverse. This took us along more interesting ridge crests on to Centrepoint Peak, and further still to reach the rocky top of Dumperfjeld. The whole outing was a very enjoyable excursion with a fascinating panorama of mountain and glacier as we climbed.

Next evening we pushed into Hole-in-the-Wall Glacier as its first-ever visitors, where we'd chosen a most appealing peak which we began to ascend by its North East Face. In our now usual roping up order we cramponned up hard ice past small rock outcrops, thinking how we could avoid this as a descent route, then pulled out right to cross a wide saddle. A final steep slope of ice led to a thinning summit ridge and the top of Majordomo Peak. It was two in the morning as we got there and the mountain was bathed in soft sunshine. Going down we retraced our steps into the wide saddle, then linking into one rope we struck off northwest to forge a trail down a long slope broken with seracs and cut by crevasses. Despite one or two deadends we dropped out onto ice and could get down onto Hole-in-the-Wall Glacier and regain our skis. At the end of this long trip we repaired into our tents at eight o'clock in the morning, but by two in the afternoon we were roasting in fierce sun, unable to sleep in the heat. The continuous light took some getting used to and tracking days was not always easy. We helped Norman to celebrate his birthday with a few drams of malt whisky, and laughed when ten minutes later he'd consulted his diary and announced that he'd missed the correct date by a whole day, so we had a few more drams to help him commiserate.

A shorter night's exercise was needed and the South Face and Ridge of Jack Tar Peak fitted the bill. We were pleasantly surprised to find a few flowers among the rocks not far below the top, although colourful lichens were not uncommon on many of the rocky sections we had climbed. With the weather set fair, we left the tents at eight on another evening and skied along West Side Glacier to the toe of a ridge bounding the rumpled face of a big peak. By a combination of steep rises on the left side and

more defined sections of crest we climbed up this Starboard Ridge, past midnight and on into the next morning. We picked a way through a short band of loose rock to the final ridge of Anchorman Peak. The highest point was one of a number of large rock pinnacles, all being piles of precariously perched basalt blocks which we chose not to disturb, sitting just beneath them in windfree sunshine to take in the huge outlook. This sense of space stayed with us on the descent and pleasant ski back to camp.

Later that day the sky clouded over from the northeast and a wind sprang up. We awarded ourselves a night off, which was just as well since snow started to fall and drift round the tents. By midnight the camp area was plastered with fresh wet snow and so were the mountains. All through the day the wind blew, uncomfortable and cold, so we banked some more sleep and husbanded our strength. A few hours on and Rob reported calm air and clear sky, so we decided to capitalise on the refreshed surfaces by going out for another ski tour. Soon we were making to the east along Broadway, covering five kilometres in an hour. Turning southeast we skied up to a shallow col in a ridge where we were overflown by a single glowing white bird which circled twice to look at us before flying west. It gave us the name for our col, Ivory Gull Pass, from where we'd seen over to another big glacier system and yet more impressive peaks. Two hours of pleasant skiing saw us back to camp pondering our next moves. In the event our very next attempt to climb petered out in unhealthily warm weather as we stood beneath a big north face bergschrund in the first bay of West Side Glacier.

With a mix of disappointment and reluctance we walked away from it. But the next mountain along was soon to provide us with the finest climb of the whole expedition. For a start it was the best looking peak in the area and its long North Ridge was the most appealing, aesthetic line we could wish for. We were all eager to try it. Shortly before nine of an evening we were away to ski round to the foot of the ridge where we stopped to gear up. The very end of the arête was a rock buttress which we avoided on the right, where, taking the lead myself, I sought a line slanting up across ice to aim for the crest. This involved crossing several crevasses of unknown magnitude, made more disconcerting by the very discomforting sounds of water running into unseen depths. Higher up there were more crevasses with very insecure snowbridges which we crossed by actually crawling over them,

Descent from Jack Tar Peak

The author on top of Jack Tar Peak *Photo: Sandy Gregson*

Narwhal Tooth Peak from the northeast on Broadway Glacier

with knees punching holes right through in places. Running out a full ropelength I managed to get lodged into an ice moat at the top of the slope where I could reach rocks to place safe anchors. The others quickly joined me, and as midnight ticked by I offered Norman the lead, handing him a bunch of wired nuts. These I had carried on all of our climbs, in spite of some gentle mockery from my friends, as they'd hardly been used.

The lower ridge was dotted with outcrops and pinnacles and as I followed with Graham and Sandy, I was amused to find that Norman had decorated each awkward step with a nut runner for protection. Further up, the ridge narrowed and changed direction with a succession of superb ice arêtes, sweepingly exposed. Norman had dodged onto either side as necessary and sometimes trod the precise crest duckfoot fashion. This was magnificent climbing with massive drops on both sides, and we looked up to the steepening final arête merging into the convex head of the mountain and so to its summit. Norman, careful all the way, placed a series of ice screws to safeguard our final progress up the steep slope to the small summit area. As we all gathered there, we felt a great sense of satisfaction after such a fine piece of mountaineering, the first ascent of Harpoon Ridge to the top of Narwhal Tooth Peak, our highest point.

The views in the early morning sunshine were stunning, but soon a cold wind began to chill us and push our minds to focus on descent. We wanted to make a full traverse of the peak by going down the West Ridge so re-ordered our rope positions to make best use of our experience and skills. The way down was an interesting line itself, steep and with some exposure, forming a fine counterpoint to our ascent route, but we were able to move together for the most part. Losing height quickly, we eventually traversed horizontally through a small notch in the ridge to recross onto the West Side Glacier. Once more on safe ground we stopped to eat and drink, enthusing about our route. As we strode back beneath the mountain's imposing North West Face we felt very happy with our night out, winding our way back to camp in great contentment.

Now only a few days remained until our skiplane pick-up was due, but we felt we could still fit in a couple of outings. Four of us went back over the glacier to Outlook Col where we made a simple climb by a zigzag route to the summit of Farawa Peak. On return to camp everyone was satisfied

The first ascent of Harpoon Ridge on Narwhal Tooth Peak *Photo: Sandy Gregson*

Climbers on the upper section of Harpoon Ridge, Narwhal Tooth Peak

with the climbing we'd managed to do, so favour fell on the suggestion to try to get up onto the edge of the Inland Ice. It would be a chance to get a sensation of that enormous expanse of white space beyond the horizon of dark mountains that bounded our base camp views. Leaving the tents at nine in the evening we skied lightly laden onto the West Side Glacier making good time past the toe of Harpoon Ridge, halting an hour later by Starboard Ridge where we ate and drank before fitting skins to our skis. Turning the corner of Anchorman Peak we started the prolonged climb to the head of the glacier beneath some nice peaks. As the gradient increased we found a way round a zone of large crevasses and just after midnight pulled into the easing of Col Beyond, wary of a corniced edge guarding a long drop ahead of us. A mass of peaks came into view extending along the enormity of the Sortebræ Glacier system. The wind from the north strengthened and blew very cold, chilling to perhaps minus 25 degrees Celsius as we hurried into jackets and took a few photographs. Time to go. Skiing down was quick, spoiled only by the arrival of cloud across the sky and we reached the camp again after a six-hour round trip. Now we had a weekend in which to sort and repack our kit in time for the pick-up, but we found ourselves under less than encouraging weather with grey skies and some further snowfall. Expecting the aeroplane in another twenty four hours we crept into sleeping bags to keep warm in the evening. Less than half an hour later came the unmistakeable drone of engines and to our great surprise the Twin Otter appeared, circled over the camp and swooped in to land, causing us to scramble back into clothes. The pilot, grinning, explained that more bad weather was on its way, so he'd pushed his schedule to lift us out before we might be blocked. We rushed to get the tents down and cram our gear into the aircraft then a swift take off bore us up into the air to head off out to the coast to fly over the sea directly to Akureyri in northern Iceland. Two hours later we landed and the duty-free shop was opened specially for us, so soon we were disposing of a succession of celebratory beers.

2001 TANGENT EXPEDITION TO THE RIGNYS BJERG MOUNTAINS
Norman Vernon, Rob Mac Callum, Graham Poole, Dave Rothery, Sandy Gregson and Jim Gregson

Descent of the West Ridge of Narwhal Tooth Peak

Looking northwest from Champs-Elysées Glacier

15 Under Arctic Sky

The treasure that is William Scoresby's *An Account of the Arctic Regions* has rightly been called the foundation stone of Arctic science and even for today's reader it provides so much to help reinforce the experiences and sensations of travel in the far North. The observant visitor can find much fascination in the old whaling captain's descriptions and explanations of many striking phenomena.

Some of the optical effects to be seen in the atmosphere at high latitudes make at times a vivid and impressive backdrop to the expedition experience. On numerous occasions, on a high glacier or at the fringes of the Inland Ice of Greenland I have gazed in wonder at those curiosities which go by the name of "sundogs." These are also known as parhelia or mock suns, appearing as two bright spots on either side of the true sun, creating that eerie and strange illusion of three objects all in the sky at once. Quite often they are seen together with a halo round the sun, the two features being produced under similar conditions. When sunlight passes through a thin layer of ice crystals, either in cirrus cloud or falling at lower levels, sundogs may form if the usually hexagonal ice crystals are oriented horizontally with their large flat sides facing downwards. They can even take on delicate colour tints but more often only their brightness brings them to the observer's attention.

When able to look across the cold waters of Arctic seas, it is not uncommon to become aware of that other apparent oddity of the North, the superior mirage. From camps on the shores of Scoresbysund I have often stared at what seems impossible to the logical mind. Huge icebergs appear to float suspended in the sky, above the horizon of vast chilly waters. These shimmering castellated images seem to defy reality.

They are caused when colder, denser air at the ocean surface is overtopped by warmer layers heated by the sun. Light reflected upwards is then refracted back down by the warm layer so it leads the viewer to see inverted images of icebergs projected into the sky above. This effect adds to and emphasises the magic of experiencing the Arctic at first hand. The privilege of visiting these very special wild places is borne directly onto the retina. The natural world reveals another of its wonders and one sits in awe before it, happy to be there in one of Earth's compelling regions.

16 A Different View of the High Arctic

Trekking in Milne Land, East Greenland

The ice-planed rock of the convex slabs swept down into the limpid water of the mountain tarn. As we traversed along, just a few metres below us gently paddled two decoratively plumaged Great Northern Divers. These beautiful black and white flecked birds displayed no fear as they swam towards us, rather an engaging attitude of curiosity about our intrusion, as they cocked to one side their green-shot dark heads to peer at us with glittering red eyes. Perceiving no threat each bird in turn dived beneath the water surface in search of fish, propelling themselves with powerful strokes of their widewebbed, rear-set feet and legs.

Earlier in the year I had received a telephone call: "Are you interested in leading a trekking group on Milne Land?" Shelving embryonic plans for a trip to the Alps, I accepted the opportunity with some alacrity for it would take me back once more to Greenland, this time to an intriguing uninhabited island rather than the high glaciers and icecap of all my previous visits.

My small group flew first to Iceland, then next day over to Kulusuk and on northeastwards to the small airstrip at Constable Pynt. During this journey I was able to stare down at many of the peaks I had already climbed in Schweizerland, the Kronprins Frederik Bjerge, the Watkins Bjerge and the Rignys Bjerg mountains, trying to decide if I was seeing any real effects of global warming. At Constable Pynt, a dusty gravel strip bulldozed onto a wide delta in Jameson Land, we collected pre-freighted food and equipment and bumped along by pick-up truck to a rudimentary jetty on the shore of Hurry Fjord. Here we transferred our rucksacks and boxes into first an open boat, then onto a motor launch bobbing offshore among the floes of broken pack ice.

Milne Land lies on latitude 70 degrees North, an island itself about the size of Yorkshire enclosed inside the gigantic fjord system of Scoresbysund – Kangertitivaq – said to be the world's largest. Huge glaciers born in the Inland Ice calve icebergs into this inlet whose tidewater is frozen over for more than half the year, so we had no real idea how long our coming voyage might take. We needed to cover about 200 kilometres, first travelling south through Hurry Fjord then rounding Kap Stewart to go west right across Hall Bredning, the central reach of Scoresbysund, to get to our intended landing in Blanke Bugt on the southern coast of Milne Land. We were rather surprised by the speed of travel adopted by our boatman, a young Inuit who spoke decent English. The unpainted stainless steel hull of the motor launch bounded through the cold but calm waters in tandem with the open, outboard-powered boat piloted by the young man's father. This second vessel also carried two Inuit women and an array of large fuel jerrycans.

As the journey progressed we met zones of pack ice which necessitated some impressive slalom sailing to thread safe passage. Only once did we find ourselves in a cul-de-sac causing a retreat and a major re-direction. We headed west into bright sunshine with Milne Land forming a growing silhouette across the horizon. Wherever there was ice in the water we saw hundreds of Little Auks or Dovekies in flocks of varying sizes. These small birds took frenziedly to the wing at the approach of the boats, in a frantic whirr of black and white, with many of them dropping back into the water after short distances to then panic-dive as the vessels overran them. As far as we could tell most of them bobbed safely back up in our wake.

Arabertoppe and The Prow above Vinkeldal, Milne Land

Beach camp at Blanke Bugt, Milne Land

Boat journey west through Scoresbysund to Milne Land

Somewhere in the middle of Scoresbysund the boats hove to in order to refuel the motors. This involved manhandling a couple of the fifty-litre jerrycans from the open boat into the launch to allow a siphoning process into the fuel tanks.

Milne Land filled the sky as we drew by Kap Leslie, its easternmost point. From there we ran parallel to the coast, curving round large icebergs to finally make our way slowly into Blanke Bugt. The proposed landing having been chosen from an inadequate map and a confusing aerial photograph, we were curious to see how we might get ashore. This manoeuvre involved another transfer back into the open boat for a careful nosing onto a boulder and gravel beach where a mostly dryshod landing and unloading could be effected. To our surprise the boat journey had only taken five hours from start to finish, whereas we had anticipated a much longer, slower chug. We quickly scribbled a note detailing the date for our pick-up then thanked the boatmen and waved them off on their return to their village at Ittoqqortoormiit. As the late evening chilled, but didn't darken, we located a reliable water supply and selected a viable campsite only fifty metres from the tideline, setting our tents onto fine gravel and moss.

Warm sunshine brought us from our sleeping bags quite early next morning, to breakfast before a wide vista of ocean, iceberg, glacier and mountain. We had in front of us twelve days to explore and investigate our surroundings, and having deliberately eschewed technical climbing were unburdened by gear and weight. Above us rose the peaks of the Arabertoppe, and past them the enormous trench of Vinkeldal curling its braided channels enigmatically across the map. This colourful chart also promised numerous tarns and lakes, but with a scale and contour interval which rendered it less than ideal for accurate navigation. Our intention had been to move camp further inland, to get nearer to the mountains and further from the mosquitoes! A first day's exploration led us to revise this plan: reasonably level campsites and decent water supplies proved to be incompatibly available, except by chance at our landing beach, so we decided to stay there and opt for slightly longer days out. We were armed with a rifle to counter any possible Polar Bear threat, but in high summer these animals tend mostly to be out on the pack ice hunting for seals so we found there to be more risk from mosquito bites than from higher up the food chain.

Each day we would set off inland or along the coast, investigating the fascinating complexities of the landscape. The geology and the landforms made a dense puzzle which we tried to unravel as we went along. We were amazed and delighted by the variety in the flora, with the keen botanists in the group eventually claiming firm identification of over ninety species of flowers, grasses, sedges, ferns and dwarf tree types. This unexpected richness added colour to the land and a pleasant contrast to the expanses of bare rock and scree of the higher ground. Bird life too, was abundant in numbers and more than twenty species were observed. Mammals were less in evidence although we had sightings of Arctic Fox, Lemmings and a delightful young Stoat. Many Reindeer antlers were seen but their owners are no longer roaming this area. Dessicated droppings suggested the presence of Musk Ox and Arctic Hares but we did not meet them. The terrain for our walks and scrambles was varied and at times arduous and difficult to negotiate. If we followed a river or stream we would go from gravel to boulder fields, from mossy tundra to enormous tussocks. When going up onto ridges we walked over and through dwarf willow and birch, ground mantled with bilberry, crowberry and bearberry plants, then acres of bare ice-smoothed and polished rock slabs. Granitic domes and outcrops gave elevated viewpoints, with many examples of apparent overflow channels carved across the grain of current drainage patterns: curiously many of these channels were floored with remarkably level natural cobbled paving. The numerous lakes and tarns lay in solid rock basins, or were held in by moraine dams. Eskers and drumlins, stone polygons and stripes, striations in the rock, erratic boulders – all bore witness to successive phases of glaciation as well as that currently in progress.

We were very much cheered by the presence of so many birds. Barnacle and Pink-Footed Geese were obviously prolific breeders: both species seemed to operate a crèche system for the care of unfledged goslings, moving on foot to water when disturbed, with other groups of feeding adults flying off to maintain comfort zones. Moulted feathers and eggshell fragments dotted the tundra. We often saw Arctic and Long-tailed Skuas, Eiders and Long-tailed Ducks, Red-throated and Great Northern Divers. Along shorelines flew Arctic Terns, Iceland and Glaucous Gulls. On the beaches ran Turnstones, Dunlin and Ringed Plovers. In the hills we watched Ptarmigan and their young, Wheatears and Snow Buntings, while Ravens flew overhead. The colour and greenery of the tundra vegetation, together with several types of fungi supported insect life other than the mosquito. Spiders, moths and some butterflies also made themselves visible.

We climbed a number of small hills and rocky tops, often to get high enough to see the terrain as a "real map", to allow us to work out approaches to the two major features, Vinkeldal and the basalt-capped Arabertoppe mountains. Vinkeldal forms a huge trough incised deep into the bedrock of Milne Land, not now filled with ice but still channeling massive drainage from the island's own icecap. At its seaward end Vinkeldal is tidal for several kilometres. One day we walked out on its delta until stopped by a deep water channel: a little further out sat a group of huge grounded icebergs. Turning inland we had to climb onto a rocky ridge to avoid mudflats and sandbars which flooded at high tides. Never less than a couple of kilometres wide, this major drainage system seems to have been ice-carved into hard, resistant rock, with a noticeable change in geology to its east where we could see in the distance much gentler country than where we explored.

Much further inland, the many braidings of the Vinkeldal river are forced into only one channel where a sill of extra hard rock floors the valley. We were able to forge a descent here and found ourselves alongside a raging cataract. Millions of tons of water roared through a slot gorge and poured in a seething brown-grey torrent down a waterfall over the rock sill. The valley sides below here were formed by a loose alluvial fill swirled by the wind: probably the remains of an ice-dammed lake bed. We scrambled up slabs above the cataract to reach a vantage point looking further into upper Vinkeldal, each side here formed by cliff and sweeps of scree or moraine. A huge prow of rock projected from the Arabertoppe peaks. This was some impressive raw landscape.

Our first attempt to get higher on the Arabertoppe mountains was slowed by the incredible roughness of the ground and we met more difficulties than anticipated. Dead ground meant we became involved in some very tiring work over unstable boulder fields and progress was not rapid. Binocular views in any case showed that we would probably not get to any main summit but we wanted to get as high as possible. This early probe was useful reconnaissance so on another day we pushed uphill on a more propitious route, working up through a geological rainbow. Eventually we even left behind most of the vegetation as we ascended steep slopes of fine gravel scree, bands of basalt and odd intrusions of brightly coloured rock. As we came over an intermediate ridge we accepted that we couldn't get onto the final few hundred metres of the Arabertoppe. Above us the peaks were capped by alternating tiers of very steep scree and vertical loose basalt. Nearer the summits the rock bands held huge pinnacles of columnar brown stone. We traversed along the intermediate crest, enjoying views west to the Gaaseland peninsula, south to the mainland behind Volquart Boons Kyst, and down to the icebergs in the sounds around Milne Land. The colouration of the rock astounded us, testament to its formation and alteration by extremes of heat and cold. Descent back to camp at the coast took us down through more of this fascinating landscape.

As our time ran down we relaxed and felt contented. We'd had only one day and night of poor weather, with rain. The mosquitoes hadn't been too voracious most of the time! The area we had explored had been very interesting to investigate. A satellite phone call to confirm our boat pick-up for the next day hinted at a possible time delay as onshore winds had apparently pushed a lot of sea ice back into Scoresbysund from the open sea. The following morning we could see for ourselves: the water between us and the mainland now held many more substantial icebergs, with the promise of some exciting sailing. Several hours later than hoped for the boats came into view, tiny against the ice. It didn't take long to load and transfer onto the silver-grey motor launch which then turned east to sail away from Milne Land. The size and number of icebergs gave a very impressive reiteration of our location ih the High Arctic as we snaked through the open leads. Massive blocks of ice glistened and towered over the boats which had to butt into a heavy chop caused by strong easterly winds, so there was a big contrast to our inward voyage. This journey out was much noisier and rougher, and enlivened at one point by a huge berg rolling over in a complete capsize as we passed by not so far away.

There was time to reflect on the trip. The good, stimulating company. The fascination of the landscape. The sheer scale of Vinkeldal. The dance of icebergs in the sea. The person who actually swam in the same cold water. The haunting calls of the divers. The quicksilver darting of the Stoat around our feet. The brokenwing distraction display of the Ringed Plover. The inaccessibility of the mountains. The flaming pink colour of "Niviarsiaq", the willowherb which is Greenland's national flower. The sunshine all through the night. The boatman finally put us ashore once more at Constable Pynt where we camped for a last night on the tundra. Even the minor drama of a lost passport – which was found less than one hour before final call – while we waited for our flight back to Iceland didn't really cast a cloud over a visit to a truly wild place.

JULY-AUGUST 2005 MILNE LAND, EAST GREENLAND
Rory Newman, Sue Thomason, Rosemary Scott, Sandy Gregson and Jim Gregson

Icebergs aground at Sandodden, Milne Land

Musk Ox – *Umimmak* Photo: Mihály Samu

17   Meeting the Residents

Encounters with wildlife or the world of nature are rare once one is high on glacier or icecap some distance inland from the Greenland coast. The enchanting exception is that the climber may still marvel at the discovery of vividly coloured flowers and lichens on the mountains, running out their lifecycles in seemingly unfavourable conditions.

Sightings of birds and mammals are much more uncommon, although I have seen Arctic Foxes nosing about at glacier camps, and been delighted by visitations from Ivory Gulls many tens of kilometres away from the sea. There are places where these startlingly white, almost luminous, birds nest far from the risks of predation, and as they are known scavengers perhaps the attractions of a colourful camp are enough to bring them close in the hope of securing food.

But there can be exceptions, and scary ones, too. Friends of mine had a salutary and unnerving experience near the end of a winter trip into the high Watkins Bjerge of East Greenland. They were in camp celebrating their first winter ascent of Gunnbjørns Fjeld, at an altitude of over 2,000 metres and in excess of 50 kilometres from the coast, waiting for a pick-up by skiplane. During their final evening they heard noises outside their tents, and were shaken to find that they were being visited by a Polar Bear. This magnificent beast, obviously hungry and a long way from any contact with its natural prey was insistent in its intentions. Lacking firearms in this instance, my friends had to resort to frantic methods of scaring the bear away, which they only managed to do after the sizeable animal had inflicted considerable damage onto several tents. Needless to say, the party did not relax into sleep for the remainder of the night: a memorable finale for their expedition.

Travels in the Arctic at the height of the brief northern summer in locations closer to the coast are much more likely to make contact with the fauna and flora which take advantage of the intense period of constant daylight and usually sustained sunlight for the vital breeding phases of their lifecycles. I had never seen the Little Auk until I made long open-boat journeys through the pack ice inside the huge extent of Scoresbysund, when for hour after hour hundreds of these black and white birds flew and dived to distance themselves from the disturbance of motorboat engine noise.

Explorations also took me into the breeding grounds of other species. Barnacle Geese which migrate for the winter to western Scotland come in early summer to breed in northeast Greenland. Wherever we walked there was evidence of moulting and eggshell fragments, and the birds exhibited two interesting behaviour patterns. Adults engaged in supervision of goslings as yet not fully fledged and thus incapable of flight, would keep their charges close to bodies of water. On becoming aware of human presence the geese would shepherd their young into the water to swim to safety. Stalking Arctic Foxes would also trigger this movement. By contrast, groups of grazing geese, always consisting of adult birds only, would have a few sentry individuals. These would give loud vocal alarm when approached to a critical distance, whereon a whole flock would take to the wing to relocate some distance away.

Eiders operated their crèche systems for communal care of their ducklings, as also did Long-tailed Ducks, almost always on saltwater. Along shorelines scurried Ruddy Turnstones and Ringed Plovers, frequently showing distraction behaviour feigning broken wing injury and deliberate tumbling action, indicating the proximity of eggs or young.

The Arctic Tern is much more likely to indulge in divebombing swoops to show disapproval of close approach, and a similar threatening tactic is adopted by the much larger and heavier Glaucous Gull.

Sightings of raptors are somewhat rarer, but good fortune may bring to view Peregrine Falcons and the powerful Gyrfalcon. The piratical methods of the Arctic and Long-tailed Skuas may also be seen. Perhaps more memorable is the strikingly patterned Great Northern Diver, a large bird with stunning plumage. Above a beautifully chequered black and white body the adult bird holds a greenblack head with a sharp, heavy bill. The dark neck sports bands of vertical striping white against black, and close views reveal the vivid red iris of alert eyes. I have been very lucky at mountain lakes to have these wonderful birds swim very close to investigate my intrusion and dive unconcernedly only a few metres away from me. The haunting modulated wailing call of this diver is one of the most evocative sounds to be heard, carrying for some distance across the tundra landscape emphasising its wildness.

Although the Arctic Fox, the Stoat, Arctic Hare and the Lemming add interest to a visit, something special is experienced when one comes into the presence of the almost prehistoric Musk Ox, so unmistakeable with long straggling hair, rather short legs and huge horns. Naturally suspicious and a little nervous, Musk Oxen must be respected and not approached too closely for fear of provoking a charge. When in groups, these bulky creatures if perceiving a threat will form a horns-out circle, or a tight shoulder to shoulder line, shielding any young animals. They watch intently, with a hard and steady stare and it is wise to give them a wide berth. They have a remarkable turn of speed and the sheer bulk of large bulls commands repect.

Moving around in complex country, it is well to anticipate that Musk Ox encounters may occur. Where populations are relatively high evidence of their presence is common: hoofprints, droppings and well-used tracks may be seen. The long hair and luxurious soft underfleece is snagged off onto vegetation and rocks used as rubbing posts. I have had some rather tense confrontations with large, solitary bulls, usually as a result of coming upon them suddenly in dead ground. Instead of instantly fleeing, a big heavy animal weighing some hundreds of kilos would stand its ground, pawing the earth to kick up dust and snort its displeasure at being disturbed. The sensible thing then to do is to retreat to a safer distance and allow the Musk Ox to move away. When you watch how comfortably these great beasts cope with difficult rocky ground, even on very steep slopes, you realise how important it is to allow them room to manoeuvre. They are at home and you are so very much the intruder. But what a privilege to see at close quarters these splendid living remnants of the Pleistocene which may have changed so little, if at all, since the end of the Ice Age.

Less rewarding as a personal experience are the attentions of the mosquito which can render the otherwise most idyllic surroundings mere background to a trial of individual discomfort. But even this can be pushed back into the deeper recesses of memory when set against other delights of Arctic sojourning. Better to think of the rhythmic pulsations of small jellyfish working along the cold waters of a fjord shoreline, or the elegant buccaneering flight of the Long-tailed Skua. I'm still hoping to set eyes on a live Polar Bear, so I'll obviously have to make other journeys into the Arctic.

1

2

3

4

1 Great Northern Diver (Common Loon) *Photo: Ken Canning*   2 Kulusuk island, Alpine Hawkweed, *Hieracium alpinum*   3 Polar Bear – *Nanoq* *Photo: Josef Friedhuber*   4 Stoat/Ermine in summer coat *Photo: Mihail Zhukov*

18   Two Dips in the Arctic Bran Tub

Explorations and First Ascents in the Sortebræ Ranges and on Milne Land, East Greenland

The Twin Otter skiplane jinked between banks of cloud and hopped about just above the mountain crests of the Borgtinderne. We were flying in along the line of the huge Borggraven glacier system to try to land on one of the higher feeder glaciers spilling off the Greenland icecap overlooking the Sortebræ ice streams. The poor maps available for this area bear the imprecisely defined label of Knud Rasmussens Land which confusingly crops up in several other locations, but eventually we landed and set up a base camp at 69.05 degrees North, 27.38 degrees West at an altitude of 1,840 metres. Going out from this position was a group led by Rosie Goolden which had operated for twenty days on the edges of the Inland Ice. Even after their efforts many more untouched peaks waited for the attentions of my own group of six.

In very cold wind we pitched our tents, looking forward to the weeks ahead of us. The mountains looked good and we had high hopes for making some first ascents. The mountains here lie about 90 kilometres east of Gunnbjørns Fjeld and the Watkins Bjerge, and offer many opportunities for treading new ground. Their only downside is that any rock which has to be tackled is usually loose or rotten basalt, but ridges and ice lines offer good climbing. While setting up camp, Geoff Bonney, veteran of several Greenland trips, amused us by producing from his ski bag the components of a six metre-tall flagpole which he soon had installed by his tent and from which he flew a resplendent Welsh dragon flag in honour of his home. With a chuckle he also decked his temporary glacier home with a colourful spray of artificial flowers.

During the first three days we skied up to a couple of cols, partly to spy out the lie of the land, and also to allow Bill Cunningham, our American member, to get the hang of skiing with climbing skins and learn to cope with a pulk. Wanting a longer outing fairly close to our base we skied on another day to the east of our tents, to then climb in two ropes of three up a long snow-ice slope to get up to a lofty crest. At the top of a convex swelling on this slope I was suddenly surprised to find myself staring into a deep blue crevasse, unseen from below, which caused a slowing of progress necessitating a T-axe anchor, a long and high stepping to get across, a bucket-seat stance and later a snow bollard belay to get us all up to the main ridge overlooking the next glacier arm. After all this, a forty minute procession along the exposed flank of a corniced arête, bypassing a few rock gendarmes, took us up to the summit of Surprise Peak, 2,405 metres. Grins all round, and extensive views across Sortebræ to the Rignys Bjerg peaks, Borgtinderne, Ejnar Mikkelsens Fjeld, and glinting in the far distance the icy bulk of Gunnbjørns Fjeld itself.

Happily we climbed down and wound our way back to camp. The talk now was in favour of moving the tents further down the glacier to a junction where access along a branch glacier would bring within reach a whole bunch of attractive peaks. Accordingly the next day we loaded our pulks and hauled away southwest until we discovered an ideal crevasse-free zone in which to establish Junction Camp, at the cost of losing just one hundred metres of altitude. There were some very big mountains adjacent to this camp but in the days and nights to come we were sadly to realise that all the approaches to them would require running the gauntlet of serac-infested icefalls which we felt were probably unjustifiable for us.

Junction Camp below unclimbed peaks in the Sortebræ Ranges

The Devil's Ridge and The Meringue, Sortebræ Ranges

However, there was no shortage of other feasible and attractive peaks within easy skiing distance so we had plenty to go at, and in any case even ski tours with no summits involved were in the midst of striking scenery.

Our next outing saw us skinning up the glacier, onto a broad saddle and further to the top of Devil's Dome, 2,151 metres. Opposite us, but across a drop of over one thousand metres, ran the towers and turrets of the Devil's Ridge, imposing but inaccessible. At its high end it sported a massive bulging feature we dubbed The Meringue. From our high position we could scout routes towards the Snow Castle and the eight summits of The Stegosaurus, so named by Bill. We had a fabulous ski run back down to the main glacier where I enjoyed showing Julian and Kate that telemarkers can sometimes match alpine skiers turn for turn.

Having ascertained that Stegosaurus 4 overtopped its neighbours we opted to try and claim its summit and set out the next day towing our climbing gear in our pulks for a couple of hours. Easy climbing on glacier slopes led us past some obvious crevasses to a narrow col from which the mountain reared up steeply to raise its head above us. As the most experienced man I led up on hard glassy ice until confronted by a big boss of snow where I was at first uncertain whether to go left or right. Choosing the left side, I moved up and traversed into a little notch from where the opposite side of the ridge fell vertically down a long rock face. As it happened, going left was correct, as the crest the other way was a very filigree affair and I was glad not to be on it. I fashioned the top of the big boss into a rather soft bollard for want of anything more secure and brought up the others. Julian then led up over a further snow bulge to a stance by some poor basalt and Geoff did the honours by reaching the summit at 2,255 metres to complete the first ascent of Stegosaurus 4. With a little juggling about we all made it to this exposed spot, all too aware of how we were perched above sweeping ice slopes on one side and immense rock cliffs on the other. From the snow bollard I could safeguard everyone's descent and we regained our skis in happy mood. By now I was trying to move the group on to more of a "night hours regime" for activity, for in twenty four hour daylight the sun is very hot in daytime and snow conditions suffer, but there was some reluctance or resistance from some in the group. However, I proposed a compromise with a late

afternoon start time, so we left camp the next time at 5:00 pm to go to investigate The Meringue.

It was very nice skiing up past the Devil's Dome, working out a route to go by the huge crevasses at the glacier head where the ice was pulling away from the parent mountain. The snow was softer than ideal when we reached The Meringue which seen end-on proved to be a very narrow snow edge of dubious stability. After soloing some way up I decided I didn't want to lead the others along it in this condition, so good naturedly they agreed to look for a consolation prize nearby, where we made our way more securely to the top of The Nipple, 2,189 metres. During the return to Junction Camp, Julian in a burst of over-exuberant skiing ricked his back rather badly, so when the next couple of days saw some poor weather blow in he was able to rest up. There was some snowfall and an unpleasant cold wind to contend with. One day an early attempt to build a "snowgirl" transmuted into a larger-than-lifesize sculpture exercise in which the "Madonna of the Glaciers" took form, complete with supporting sledge dog, and she stood sentinel over the camp until we departed. A couple of quick dashes back to base kept us stocked up with food and fuel to prolong our stay at Junction Camp, and we even made one abortive outing to try to climb which the weather foiled.

As the conditions continued to be unsettled and unpredictable, unlike what I have come to regard as the norm over several Greenland expeditions, Julian and Kate decided to explore further down the main glacier by making another camp. The rest of us opted to stay at Junction Camp and take our climbing chances as the weather permitted. Now we could go onto night-time climbing. Disappointingly our first attempt on a new peak saw us turned back by rotten rock after a very promising start by a long couloir giving onto a ridge. We did enjoy though, being out in the lovely slanting night sunshine which is a feature of Arctic climbing. In the morning Julian and Kate took down their tent, loaded a pulk and set off down the glacier for a few days. Later, in the early evening, Geoff, Bill, Sandy and I left to go up the branch glacier to have a look at the Snow Castle. After a couple of hours we paused to try to work out a safe way to negotiate what we called Crevasse Hollow: here a very pronounced dip in the glacier allowed much of the ice to escape over an edge into the

Skiing through Crevasse Hollow, Sortebræ Ranges

main Sortebræ system, with this flow creating a mass of extensive and enormous crevasses, spectacular to see but inimical to direct progress.

We had to go left, close under the west side peaks, but into deep and thus very cold shade. Bill, still getting used to using skins, was making slow going of it, while I was eager to get back into the sunlit areas higher up where the Snow Castle still glowed yellow. As we gained height a wind began to blow, reinforcing the chill and by the time we were in a position to rope up just below the peak there was a build-up of cloud too. The increasing gale made things very unpleasant and as we all suffered, a halt was called not far below the summit at 2,105 metres. The poor light made the return ski tricky as the wind had obliterated all signs of our approach track. With some awkwardness we eventually rediscovered a few traces of pole-plant marks and worked our way back through Crevasse Hollow. As we descended towards camp the wind mocked us by dying away, but the cloud remained in place.

A long sleep restored us and the morning and early afternoon sun saw the weather recover. Bill pressed us to go to attempt a higher peak over to the west which he had studied from an earlier ski outing. The bright and warm sunshine of the afternoon encouraged us to prepare, but Geoff, by some way our eldest team-mate, said he would stay behind in camp to rest. That left three of us to go to Bill's chosen mountain by a glacier approach as far as the foot of a long couloir. As Bill was not quite at ease with the technique of skinning uphill, Sandy and I were somewhat in front and waited until he joined us at 2,000 metres to rope up for the climb. For three hundred metres we kicked up a steepening slope over some avalanche debris in the couloir running up to a big swelling of dirty grey ice. The swelling could be outflanked on the left side on safer, less steep ground but as we headed this way the weather played us another trick. In minutes we were in gloom and thickly falling snow. Estimating that there would probably be another two hundred metres of height to gain we folded our hand and once more let the mountain win. Careful down-climbing took us back to our skis and pulk where visibilty was now very poor. Too poor, in fact, for safe skiing so we rearranged our rope and set off to walk out to the main glacier, fortunately without mishap. Once on the main ice stream we navigated back to camp using GPS and

Arriving at the summit of Stegosaurus 4, Sortebræ Ranges

Climbing in the Arctic night hours, Sortebræ Ranges

Approach to The Stegosaurus, Sortebræ Ranges

compass in the teeth of a gale to rejoin a relieved Geoff. This erratic weather was becoming a bit frustrating. After some sleep we woke to find the camp area strongly drifted up with the tents needing digging out. Later on, Kate and Julian skied back into view from their exploratory tour down the glacier and when they had reset their tent we exchanged news of our various outings.

The weather calmed down and the sun reasserted itself. We discussed the prospects for another climb or two and settled on trying to get to another of the Stegosaurus summits, No. 7, The Fin, which was a very elegant sail of snow and ice with a few rocks forming the summit. Bill was a little cross to have to go back over some known ground to get to it, but he decided to join the party. Julian, still nursing his back, would stay with Kate in camp. We left in the evening. A long glacier ramp conducted us upwards parallel to the extensive bergschrund slashing the mountain's northwest flank. At the upper end this 'schrund became a huge hole with a massive ice cliff upper wall. Luckily, just before this hole, the space was bridged and filled and we set up a solid anchor point to safeguard the crossing. The upper wall was sound ice, inspiring confidence and taking ice screws well. It became obvious that safety would lie in pitching the climb albeit at the expense of speed, but there were times when I could have all three of my companions climbing simultaneously up behind me once good anchors and stances had been built. By chance the orientation of the slope and the approach of midnight saw the sunlight slip away from us and the cold began to bite. A pitch on dinner-plating ice, protectable after some clearing off, took me up to rocks where our small selection of gear came into play. From there a long pitch reached the summit, a rock outcrop of perched blocks and rubble, set right over a vertical drop on the other side. I lashed the dross together with rope and slings, even using Geoff 's trusty original MOAC then brought up the others to share the summit at 2,275 metres.

The wind streamed spindrift off some of the neighbouring tops but distant views were clear. Gunnbjørns Fjeld and Ejnar Mikkelsens Fjeld were golden in the end of night sunshine. Going down meant re-entering the shade and the descent was a chilly business with the inevitable waits on the stances. I was certainly glad to get down past the bergschrund

The author with his sculpture, Madonna of the Glaciers

to be able to keep moving, and even more pleased to get back into the sunlight on the glacier. The Fin had given us a good climb, although Bill professed it had been one of the coldest he had experienced. After some of our earlier setbacks it was very satisfying.

Back at Junction Camp we rested and recovered, but the weather relapsed again into unpredictability. We were due to be picked up on the following Friday so on Wednesday we decided to go back up to base camp and loaded our pulks with everything that had to be moved. This meant heavy loads to haul uphill but in time we had it all lashed down and ready, so Sandy and myself adopted our doubleheaded hauling method to make the work somewhat easier. We had hoped that the weather might have allowed us to take one more summit but things moved against us and we spent Thursday in readying for our fly-out, with kit to be packed and all of our garbage to be compressed and sealed away for shipping out.

Information via satellite phone for a skiplane pick-up revealed a less than reliable weather outlook. I undertook to select and mark out a landing strip to give a visual clue in the event of marginal conditions prevailing. On the Friday morning there was blue sky and bright sunshine on our camp, but over in Iceland the air charter personnel were weighing up the wider weather picture against the flying time required. At last we were told that the plane would in fact, fly a dog-leg route to lay a depot for another group some two hundred and fifty kilometres from our location then come to collect us, with a proposed arrival time in the early evening. That left us with nothing to do but wait and watch as the weather began slowly to deteriorate through the afternoon. We had marked out the landing strip and had our VHF radio on standby. We expected the aeroplane to be coming from the southwest, just where the weather looked worst to us. By the due time we were experiencing snowfall, strong wind and very limited visibility. Thirty minutes overdue we heard engine noise from above and immediately made radio contact with the pilot. Of course, this confirmed what we already knew: a landing just now would be impossible and the aeroplane could not circle around waiting for a break. Another try would be made tomorrow. The engine noise died away leaving us in a slightly despondent gloom: the Arctic had the upper hand.

Saturday morning saw fortune smiling on us once more. The clouds had dispersed during the night allowing a hard frost to develop but bright sunshine held sway. Contact over the satellite phone gave us an ETA for 11:00 am and at 11:10 the distinctive sound of the Twin Otter broke over the ridge high in the south and VHF radio contact was resumed. The pilot confirmed that he could see the marked strip and turned to come in right on line. On the ground he told me that the snow was "sticky" and take-off would be difficult after the plane was loaded with the extra weight of our equipment and six passengers. In the event it took four or five wild runs, separated by rather worrying aborts, before the aircraft could get up enough speed to finally lift off the glacier and climb out of the mountains to head for Iceland bringing our adventure to a happy closure.

Just six weeks later I was flying in a much bigger aeroplane directly over the glacier on which we had camped, looking down at the very peaks where we had made our first ascents. None of our tracks were discernible after this time. Soon afterwards we had landed at the dusty airstrip of Constable Pynt. Here I was, back in Greenland for the second time in the same summer, leading a trekking group aiming to explore the western end of Milne Land, a big island lying deep inside the enormous fjord system of Scoresbysund. Five of us were to collect some pre-freighted food and equipment, pick up a rifle and ammunition from the airstrip manager, then meet our boatmen for the onward journey. My latest information had been to the effect that the Scoresbysund area had experienced a hard, prolonged winter and the sea ice breakup had been late in coming.

I'd expected to see the large motor launch I had travelled in before but once down by the makeshift quay the boat men told me that the state of the ice dictated that we would have to travel in three smaller open boats. As we needed to cover a crow-fly distance of more than two hundred kilometres this might not be good news. When our boxes and bags had been stowed into the the three small craft, a Zodiac type and two motorboats, Martin, the very helpful Dane from Ittoqqortoormiit in charge of operations sprang another surprise. "You will have to wear these suits to travel in the boats. Damned new regulations." he said handing us bulky red packages. These proved to be full-scale survival suits, oilrig style, with massive zippers, built-in gloves and flotation collars, and we felt rather weird as we struggled to put them on before clambering aboard the boats.

Thus at 7:00 pm we sailed away down Hurry Fjord and out into Hall Bredning, the big, open stretch of Scoresbysund, only it was not open very much. The pack ice crowded the water and it was impossible to steer a straight course so it would be two hundred plus who knows how many extra kilometres before we would be setting foot onto Milne Land. The survival suits protected us from the cold wind and the occasional dousings of salt spray but they had a downside. As time passed, condensation formed on the inside of the thick neoprene material and left one sitting in clammy dampness, while the integral gloves seemed to grip the hands into numbness. Still, our proximity to the all too obvious cold water only centimetres away made the prospect of an involuntary dip rather unwelcoming.

For some hours we sped back and forth zigzagging through the ice, disturbing the repose of hundreds of Little Auks which flew and dived to distance themselves from the noisy boats. With time we passed between Denmark Island and the tip of the Gaaseland Peninsula then began to turn into Fønfjord alongside Milne Land. Here there was less ice in the water, but true to its name this fjord was funnelling a strong wind from the west. Oddly in these surroundings this wind was noticeably warm on the face despite its origins on the icecap, but it was whipping the water into sizeable waves. Martin decided he wanted to "fly" the boat across the wave crests at high speed so the two of us travelling with him were wedged into the stern for this leg of the journey. Despite the speed, the next two hours were a very painful period of bone-jarring crashes and jumps over the water while trying to find something to grip onto to prevent going overboard. By 2:00 am on Sunday morning we were heartily glad to round the end of Bird Island guarding the little bay where we wanted to land to pass the icebergs pushed onto the shore, and step out of the boats onto the calm and blessedly static beach after seven hours afloat. Within less than one hundred metres we were setting up our tents at 70.25 degrees North 27.49 degrees West on a mix of bearberry, dwarf willow and moss, where in another thirty minutes a group of six or seven Musk Oxen of various sizes and ages wandered into view from behind a spur less than

The Hermelintop hills of western Milne Land

Brave or foolish? The author in the Arctic Ocean! *Photo: Sandy Gregson*

fifty metres from us. Once they had become aware of our presence they lined themselves up in a defensive row for a while then turned about and headed back inland. We too, turned about and headed for some sleep.

Before we woke, our boatmen had rested for a few hours and left in the early morning, having already agreed our pick-up arrangements for two weeks time. We now had before us the prospect of a fortnight's exploration over new ground in very attractive and impressive surroundings, the only fly in the ointment being the occasional depredations wrought by the mosquitoes of the Arctic high summer. Having been to Milne Land already, on a previous trip further east, I could see even from our camp area that this part of the island was very different in character. It rose inland much more steeply to more defined rocky summits separated by deeply cut valleys. Steep crags abounded and numerous tarns lay in quiet hollows.

The map we had was more or less page-of-an-atlas scale so our days were based on a "Let's investigate" approach as we tried to puzzle out the complexities of the landscape and memorise ways back to camp. We made a number of first ascents by interesting first-rate scrambles over the days and from each new high point we'd try to work out another new route to whichever tops caught our attention. Some of these summits were located above very impressive cliffs which might repay closer investigation by ambitious rock-climbers, and we had close views of some very striking sea cliffs on some coastal wanderings. The highest summits we gained also granted us extensive views over the deep straits separating Milne Land from the mainland, to gigantic glaciers shedding great icebergs into the sea, and to the wide whitenesses of the icecap and the fascinating mountains of Paul Stern Land to the west.

In the waters of Rødefjord we could look down onto the red sandstone of Red Island rising like a northern Ayers Rock straight out of the sea, and across to other areas of sandstone eroded into contorted domes and ravines over on the mainland. In the northern reaches of our explorations we found ourselves going from garnet-studded gneisses of the south to the granite areas which supported noticeably less vegetation. For those interested in geology, landforms and botany there was always something to hold one's eye: rock formations, glacier hollows, overflow channels, waterfalls, jewel-like tarns, moraines, raised beaches, mudflows, crags and cliffs, many different types of flowers, fungus, blueberries, crowberries, bearberries. The bird watcher could observe Barnacle and Pink-footed Geese, Red-throated and Great Northern Divers, Eider and Long-tailed Ducks, Ringed Plovers, Ptarmigan, Snow Buntings, Arctic Redpolls, Ravens, Peregrine Falcons, Arctic Terns and Glaucous Gulls. As for mammals there were Lemmings, Arctic Fox, bright white Arctic Hares and Musk Oxen which we saw every day. These imposing shaggy animals were usually in groups if they had young ones with them, often forming up defensively to weigh up our presence as a potential threat. We always tried to give them a wide berth, or at least a fair escape route by altering our own lines of progress. A little more worrying were encounters with very large solitary animals, presumably bulls, which we occasionally, or they us, startled by coming on them in dead ground. Sometimes they would flee: at others they stamped the ground kicking up dust with their hooves and snorting loudly at us. At such displays we found it better ourselves to give ground to these bulky specimens as we saw they commanded a very good turn of speed. There were numerous skeletal remains, so there is obviously a fair population on Milne Land. By contrast, ancient shed antlers were the only evidence of a former presence of Reindeer.

Although on this trip we were not involving ourselves in technical climbing here, though it could be found without great effort, we felt very privileged to be able to wander at will and discover all this new ground which we had to ourselves: to enjoy the wildness and quiet of the High Arctic, punctuated by the sound of waves or collapse and capsize of huge icebergs: to wonder at the colours and variety of wildlife that we found.

As our time on Milne Land ran out we hoped for a more comfortable return journey. On the appointed day for the boat to collect us we were a bit nonplussed by only sighting the open Zodiac with Martin at the helm. The large launch, he explained, was away involved in an emergency evacuation of another group elsewhere, but by travelling to Denmark Island we could later rendezvous with it for the later part of our own return. So, fortunately in very calm and smooth water, we five and our belongings could crowd into the open boat – without wearing the survival suits – and motored for just over two hours back through Fønfjord to put into the beautiful natural anchorage of Hekla Havn where in 1891-2 Lt. Carl Ryder's Danmark

Expedition had been one of the first to overwinter in East Greenland.

While waiting there for several hours we looked around the ancient Inuit house remains with their curious stone "mosaic" floor patterns until heavy rain set in and we retreated to take shelter in an abandoned cabin formerly belonging to the Northern Mining Company. At 4:00 in the morning in a slight fog, the big motor launch arrived and we were able to resume our journey towards Constable Pynt. The pack ice in Scoresbysund was still problematic and there was considerable reversing and backtracking, plus a certain amount of gentle nudging apart of the floes to win a way through to open water. All the time the wind was increasing with consequent rougher seas. By the time we rounded Kap Stewart into Hurry Fjord the waves were substantial and the boat drivers opted to take us further east to the village of Ittoqqortoormiit from where we'd have to take a helicopter transfer over to Constable Pynt. But the trip had one more unexpected excitement for us.

As we made our final run towards the mooring buoys by the village, a great commotion seemed to break out on the shore. People were running, pointing out into the water. Men were appearing with rifles, jumping into boats, firing up engines. As we got closer the reason made itself evident. A pod of Narwhals had swum into the bay. Once sighted they had sealed their own fates as a hue and cry signalled the onset of a hunt. To our great surprise our boatmen decided to join in, as the boats were used to drive the hapless creatures, forcing them to surface to blow whereupon the Inuit hunters began to shoot them. Blood sprayed and spread on the water. Boats sped back and forth, bullets flew. In a brief lull some of our party were put ashore with just two of us remaining afloat waiting for transfer to the quay. Just after we got back into the Zodiac with all our kit, a cry went up again and the boat wheeled about to go rushing round a headland where we became involved in efforts to snag a Narwhal carcass with grappling hooks to tow it ashore. After some time this was given up for a fruitless task, as other still-living whales remained to be pursued.

Eventually we were landed in a state of some bewilderment after this episode, leaving me to puzzle out how to make last-minute arrangements for helicopter shuttles across to the airstrip with enough time to catch our pre-booked flight back to Iceland to close off another adventure.

1. EXPEDITION TO THE SORTEBRÆ MOUNTAINS, EAST GREENLAND
  27 MAY - 17 JUNE 2006
Geoff Bonney, Julian Davey, Kate Keohane, Bill Cunningham, Sandy Gregson and Jim Gregson

2. TREKKING EXPEDITION TO MILNE LAND, EAST GREENLAND
  22 JULY - 6 AUGUST 2006
Adrian Hall, Doug Oppenheim, Tom Leatherland, Sandy Gregson and Jim Gregson

At Outlook Col, Rignys Bjerg area *Photo: Sandy Gregson*

Ski approach to the Snow Castle, Sortebræ Ranges *Photo: Sandy Gregson*

Inuit children at Kap Dan harbour, Kulusuk

19   You Always Hurt the One You Love

Change and the Arctic

Evidence continues to grow attesting to climate change and its effects and consequences for our planet. More worrying, the rates of change under current study suggest that the Earth's polar regions will exhibit more strikingly and more rapidly the influences of global warming if present trends are maintained.

The wondrous Arctic that those of us privileged to have visited is coming increasingly under pressure. Of course, nothing in the history of the planet is static or fixed for any region. The long fossil record for the northern areas can be read to show that in earlier times the climatic conditions have been markedly unlike those we imagine to characterise the Arctic as it has been known for hundreds of years.

Mankind inevitably, has made impacts on the Arctic, just as on other parts of the Earth's surface. This is true even of the Inuit and other northern peoples traditionally adapted to live and survive in cold environments, relying on hunting, fishing and gathering for their food supplies, although they achieved some degree of harmony with their surroundings. With the passage of time contacts with peoples from more "developed" parts of the world have brought change in their wake.

Fur-trapping, whaling, seal hunting and fishing have all been reponsible for impacting on the Arctic regions, exporting their economic benefits but generally causing a depletion or despoliation of the fauna endemic to these cold parts of the world. The efforts of polar explorers to "discover" the North certainly led to increases in geographic and scientific knowledge but not all of this growth in travel and greater contact with the indigenous populations can be said to have been beneficial. An argument can be made that if we know more about the world, the more we can learn about the importance of protecting it and of conserving it; the greater value we can place on biodiversity. The more understanding we can gain on the value of wildness and wilderness, the more likely we are to try to preserve it. And yet, even for someone who has been fortunate to make numerous visits to the Arctic, there are some pangs of conscience about what one is actually doing simply by going there.

"Leave nothing but footprints: take only photographs." A nice ideal, not really in dispute. But at the same time even this is not without impact. Groups spending time on the Greenland icecap or glaciers leave their tracks, nowadays often starting with the heavy spoor of a ski-equipped aircraft.

Ski tracks, footprints and evidence of camping places will in time be obliterated through melting, snowfall and windblown drift. Garbage can, and must, be taken out in the same way as it was of necessity taken in.

The tundra areas are perhaps more vulnerable than the ice. I have seen camping areas, over relatively few days, begin to show signs of wear and tear due to repeated trampling of feet. Short of levitation it is difficult to see how this can be avoided, although it is possible not to maintain a camp in any one location for too prolonged a period of time. It is, however, inescapable that the signs of occupation will persist for much longer than might be really desirable. Paradoxically, in some places I have been fascinated by finding remains of former Inuit campgrounds, stone circles of tent rings, mosaics of rock which perhaps had been hearthplaces, traces of former turf dwellings. They have been accepted as part of the charm of being in the Arctic.

The tracks of native fauna too, are imprinted on the land, along with skeletal remains. Antlers from long-disappeared populations of reindeer show up as markers of times past. Feathers from moulting geese, eggshells dotting the breeding grounds: all these seem to belong, to have a right to be there. But one does have a sense of unease sometimes with one's own additions or alterations to the landscape, even when they might seem innocuous. I once watched for a few days as some of my group members gathered from shorelines more and more driftwood, with talk of a cheering bonfire to mark the end of their trip. Feeling unsympathetic to this idea, in an area where scrub willow and dwarf birch struggled to grow any more than finger-thickness, I finally asked the team to forgo their planned blaze. I explained that apart from the ashes and charcoal that would result, the very timber itself had quite likely made a lengthy drift through the wastes and waters of the Arctic Ocean possibly from origins in far-off Siberia, before washing up on the Greenland shores where we stood. It was part of what we'd come a long way to experience. To their credit they agreed not to burn it, thus avoiding destroying evidence of the operation of one of the Earth's ecosystems.

Having fallen under the spell of the Arctic, it is difficult to refute arguments that each return visit chips away a little more at the fragility of the very environment that one professes to care for. I haven't been to the great rainforests, or the vast deserts of the world, but thanks to other travellers I know they are there and I accept their importance and value. By allowing some glimpses into the special places of the North maybe more people will come to believe in the worth of the world and its wildness, and the importance of not allowing it to disappear forever.

1

2

3

4

1 Kap Dan – seal meat on a drying frame   2 An old kayak frame at Kap Dan village   3 Kulusuk island – an East Greenlandic sledge   4 Inuit dog sledge team leaving Constable Pynt

20 Bright, Shining Mountains

Paul Stern Land 2008 and 2010

The tall cairn was perched on the brink of a great precipice falling from the summit of Hermelintop in western Milne Land. As our heart rates subsided we stared over the ice-pocked waters of Rødefjord to the glistening mainland beyond. The huge flows of the Vestfjord Gletscher and Rolige Bræ pushed enormous bergs into the fjord heads and out into the slow currents of the Scoresby Sund channels. Rising above the fjords we could see the gleaming flanks of higher mountains stretching towards the Inland Ice. These peaks lay in the area called Paul Stern Land and formed a tempting prospect for a future visit.

In 2007 I was busy with a ski touring trip to the northern part of Liverpool Land, so it was 2008 before the opportunity came to get a closer look at these likely virgin mountains. In the event there were just three of us able to make a group. Poor flying weather delayed us for some days at Akureyri in northern Iceland but eventually we travelled to Constable Pynt to load our kit into the Twin Otter aeroplane. The airstrip was still in the grip of an exceptional winter's snow accumulation, with the runway and apron areas ploughed clear but ankle deep in slushy mud as the spring thaw was setting in.

Our inward flight the next morning gave us some spectacular views of the Paul Stern Land mountains, especially of Arken (the Ark) isolated in a huge glacial sea and presenting a notable challenge. We were destined to land further west where a rendezvous had been negotiated with a pair of German mountaineers who had been out on the icecap for six weeks while travelling and climbing their way northwards. They had arrived in the latitude of Paul Stern Land but some way to the west on the high fringe of the Inland Ice. Here they were pinned down by a week of bad weather and running low on food and fuel needed picking up from a location which was not ideal for us.

Once down onto the ice we hastened to erect our tents to provide shelter from strong cold winds. The next day we skied up to reach the top of a nunatak from where we could prospect a route to allow us to move closer to the main mountain group. We were about 25 kilometres of crow-fly distance from the ideal position, but the nature of the glaciers would not permit us to make a direct approach. We would need to run in a big arc to the north then eastwards, rounding other nunataks before descending via the wide glacier which flows east across the north side of Paul Stern Land. This trek would involve us moving all of our food and equipment with us but we soon realised that we didn't have the pulk capacity to shift everything at once. Sandy would have to shoulder quite a heavy rucksack load, while Geoff and myself pondered the size of pulk burdens we could manage. As we built the loads we accepted that we would need to do some relaying with the inevitable slowness of forward progress interrupted by backtracking to bring up the surplus quantities.

An interim camp was made on the icecap edge so that Sandy and I could return to the landing zone for a second load. After some hours' sleep we decided for the next leg to place a forward depot as the ice surface became a sea of sastrugi. We then pressed ahead, descending to the northeast for about ten kilometres onto a much flatter part of the glacier where we could set a camp. After the double journey to pick up the heavy items from the forward depot we agreed that more days of heavy pulk

Norlandair's Twin Otter on arrival in Paul Stern Land

On the summit of Ararat – Paul Walker and the author *Photo: Sandy Gregson*

hauling and relaying might not be the best way of using our time. Geoff, in particular, being a few years older, was not keen on wearing himself out as a beast of burden. We thus decided to make our main base at this camp and accept slightly longer ski approaches to the mountains, when we would only be conveying climbing equipment. Also, this location would be perfect for our final aircraft pick-up as there would be ample landing area whatever the wind direction might be. The only drawback to the campsite was the soon to be evident fact that it lay squarely in the track of almost constant katabatic windspill off the icecap which manifested itself as cold westerly winds bringing great quantities of spindrift.

We awoke from a lengthy period of much needed sleep to find the tents severely drifted up and other kit almost buried. Geoff, drawing on his vast desert experience, suggested that we needed to modify the drifts into classic sand dune forms with a steep scarpface behind the tents, falling away into a smooth convex windward face. With trial and error we eventually got these "snow dunes" to work well in diverting drift to either side of the tents. For more efficiency, Geoff also built a system of "wind splitters" – small triangular section pillars of snow a short distance upwind of the protective dunes. These worked remarkably well in deflecting spindrift away from the camp and thus life at Camp Venturi, as we called it, became more bearable, although never becoming a shirt sleeve resort such as we've had in other regions.

Time now to consider some climbing. Sandy pointed out that the higher summits at the western end of the northern nunatak zone were closer than the peaks in the southern group so we decided to look at these first. For an initial outing we skied northeast for a couple of hours onto a higher icecap shelf. There, at the foot of a long slope of glasslike bare blue ice we donned crampons to ascend to a final rocky summit. Geoff with his keen geologist's eye showed us that the rocks were studded with garnets, hence we arrived at the name of Garnet Dome for this top. Eager to gain a higher vantage point we decided to cross a glacial saddle to the southeast to climb up to the next mountain on its icy North West Face to find a way along some rocky ribs to the summit crest. At the highest point we constructed a cairn and rested a while to study the lie of the land. From this top, Peak Emyr, we worked out a feasible route

of approach which we could use to get to Ararat, the obviously highest summit in this area, which we could tackle on another occasion. Looking out towards Arken and the very tempting group of main peaks, we began to realise and accept that our camp was sited just a little too far away for ski approaches to be manageable in sensible times – the cost of our rendezvous with the Germans. Back in camp the wind blew fiercely for a day or two deterring us from action, but once fully rested we set about aiming to climb Ararat. We skied away to the east, passing through a crevassed area then descending slightly on very rough ice to the base of Peak Emyr. From here we were able to make a diagonal ascending traverse over loose rocks to gain a footing on the south-facing ice slopes of Ararat. Moving up and on into the more cheering night-time sunshine from the north we worked onto a crest of rock steps, then up once more to get onto the corniced snow arête which brought us to the summit of Ararat. The outlook to the north over the nunatak zone and distant Saven range was stunning.

Turning to the south we studied Arken, a much more problematic-looking peak, and enjoyed a grandstand view into the heart of Paul Stern Land where we were able to identify what would be an ideal base location for a possible future visit. Content with our first ascent of this highest peak we left to go down. As the descent progressed the wind began to increase in strength. Lower down we stopped to eat and put on extra clothing, before hurrying down to where we'd left our skis. The return to Camp Venturi was something of a struggle, directly into the teeth of a shrieking gale with face-stinging spindrift to add to the discomfort. Looking directly upwards revealed blue sky, but visibility ahead was severely impeded by the head-high driven snow. Steering by compass and using a distant nunatak as a navigation beacon we forced our way back to camp, but only regained sight of the tents from a very short distance away. Thankfully we tumbled into their shelter. Sandy then alerted me to my ice-coated face. I'd had great difficulty getting the hood of my jacket to stay in place on the return journey and was now to pay the price in the form of a frost-nipped cheek. This required careful rewarming and future care, but some skin was lost in the next two days. We'd had a very good climb, but needed our experience and resilience to get back safely to camp.

The continuing winds allowed us to stock up on sleep but ate into our remaining time. We ruled out the long approaches to the main group of peaks and in the end had to settle for a trip in the opposite direction – to the beacon mountain at the very threshold of the icecap. Geoff, perhaps still tired from Ararat, did not come, so with Sandy I skied out to this Windscoop Beacon, named for the great deep bowl round its rocky foot. We gained access to it from the west, climbing rocks to its top, then seeing it had a twin summit traversed to take that one also. In deteriorating weather we returned to Geoff in Camp Venturi, still hoping for one more outing. Disappointingly we didn't get the chance as the date for our pickup approached. Needless to say, the morning that the Twin Otter flew in was marked by flawless sky and brilliant sunshine.

As we flew back to the airstrip at Constable Pynt we gazed over Paul Stern Land and wondered about the possibility of making a return visit at some time to get more closely to grips with those shining mountains. While we were cooling our heels at the airstrip, another group of British climbers were starting their own climbing period among the northern nunataks. We later learned that they had reached a dozen or more new summits as well as repeating a couple of our own climbs. The weather was more benign than that we'd endured.

Further researches once we were back home shed a little more light onto the history of Paul Stern Land. The area was visited from the south by geologists in 1958, when the peak named Sfinks (Sphinx) was climbed. Paul Stern himself was a member of this group. He was a Swiss geologist of Dutch descent who had taken part in a number of geological field expeditions to northeast Greenland in the late 1950s. Sadly he was killed in the Swiss Alps in 1959 in a stonefall accident. His geology colleagues applied to have his name commemorated in the official place-name record hence Paul Stern Land appears on the map. Later geological groups also named some of the other peaks in the region, although they remained unclimbed. Although we had thought ourselves to be the first climbers to be active in the area, our searching in other records revealed that two British military groups had accessed the eastern end of Paul Stern Land by boat approach through Vestfjord. In 1978 the first of these teams made a few ascents adjacent to the Rolige Bræ, and in 1987 a second group of soldier mountaineers repeated two of these climbs and added five more, although none of these were in the central part of the district.

Having seen for ourselves the very attractive reservoir of still unclimbed peaks we resolved to try to return. As we laid plans in early 2010, Geoff confirmed his interest in coming back, and our friend Paul Walker would join us. A little later we were contacted out of the blue by Willem-B. Stern from Switzerland. He had become aware of our report from 2008 and was intrigued, as he is the surviving brother of Paul Stern. In correspondence he was able to give us more information about his deceased brother's activities in Greenland and eventually disclosed that he'd long harboured a wish to see in person the area that bore his brother's name. We asked him if he might be interested in joining our own group as our plans were fairly advanced and to our delight he agreed to team up with us – despite a little misgiving over his age (70) and his lack of ski experience. Our number grew to six with the addition of Robin Collins, who was willing to travel all the way from Australia to join us. The three of us from 2008 plus the three extras for 2010 gave us a splendid combined age of 367 years, a truly vintage team.

As our plans crystallised towards final form during the late winter of 2010, Iceland's volcano Eyafjallajökull burst into eruption, causing widespread disruption of air travel over Europe. We followed its continuing discharge of ash as the dates for our own travel neared. Fortunately at the due flight days the ash problem had blown away towards Svalbard in the northeast as the winds changed direction and we were all able to gather in Reykjavík as intended. A day later we flew across the pack ice in the Denmark Strait and into the airstrip at Constable Pynt. Here the newly repainted Twin Otter skiplane was waiting and after a short time we were ready to go. There followed a breathtaking journey in brilliant visibility, first across the snowy billows of Jameson Land then the billiard table smooth frozen sea of Hall Bredning, Scoresby Sund before running the length of the fantastic landscape of Milne Land. We then flew in over the Vestfjord to approach Paul Stern Land by heading up over Døde Bræ with the enormous Rolige Bræ to our right.

Our pilots firmly declined our first choice of landing area, right in the centre of Paul Stern Land, mindful of the fact that in recent years their very same aeroplane had become stuck on the ground in very soft snow conditions on a few occasions, involving complicated and costly retrieval operations. We had to agree to a slightly more distant landing zone out on the more open reaches of the upper Døde Bræ, so flanking the big peak of Arken we banked for a close inspection before touching down at 1,540 metres about 4 kilometres northwest of Bændelbjerg.

Quickly we unloaded our kit from the Twin Otter as the pilots were keen to be on their way home all the way to Iceland. Once the aircraft had left we pitched our tents and settled into camp. The next day, in warming sunshine we took stock of our location, made our dispositions in respect of equipment and agreed a plan of action. Eager to be active we decided that on this very evening we would ski off a little to the south and try to climb to some attractive summits along a ridge which would afford an overview of the area. As we gained height the snow improved and we progressed without incident to a fine rock buttress marking the prominent top of Copper Knob at 1,890 metres. We erected a cairn using rocks peppered with many garnets. As we did this, three large geese flew past close by, calling as their wingbeats powered them along. Perhaps they were vanguards of this season's returning breeding migrants? Tracing a way down the slabby crest of Copper Knob we arrived at a saddle from which a beautifully sinuous corniced arête led us up over the snowy head of the rounded Weisskopf at 2,000 metres, then further as midnight passed, onto the long slope leading up to the projecting brown rocks marking the summit of Peak Bruno, 2,050 metres. We were pleased to have secured three first ascents from this first outing, descending happily in lovely raking light to eventually ski very rapidly back to camp over the now-frozen snow.

After some well-earned sleep we now loaded the pulks for our intended major move into the central part of Paul Stern Land. This would clearly be heavy work, and our elevated position of the night before had revealed to us that the glaciers were more crevassed than had been apparent two years ago. As the evening cooled we drew away from our first camp area, leaving a depot of food and fuel against our later return. Slowly we moved to the southeast passing below the beautiful peak of Bændelbjerg to lose some height before turning south to seek a route into the heartland glacier. Passing some moraine bands and a mostly frozen meltwater pool

Ararat from the ridge of Peak Emyr, Paul Stern Land

Arken (The Ark) from Camp Katabat, looking east

Looking north from the summit of Ararat during the first ascent in 2008. Time – midnight

we now had to make a lot of height over much steeper ground. The pulk hauling became ever more arduous, laden as we were with equipment and supplies for ten or twelve days. To frustrate our intentions we now encountered a closely spaced and unsuspected grid of crevasses impeding our progress. Photographs from 2008 had suggested a problem-free route, but that year we'd arrived after a very heavy snowfall winter. Now all was different. Paul and I went ahead to scout the way, crossing numerous thinly bridged crevasses. Reluctantly we eventually concluded that these would become a much greater problem for our eventual return as seasonal melt-out nowadays gains pace at a phenomenal rate as the Arctic, in our experience, is warming up at a much faster pace in recent years.

Naturally, our companions were disappointed as we conveyed our judgement to them, for we had all hoped to be able to get right in amongst the attractive peaks that distinguish Paul Stern Land. We counselled a short retreat back a little way along Døde Bræ to a fine location fairly close to the toe of Bændelbjerg's northwest ridge. This took another ninety minutes of hard work until we stopped to establish what became known as Camp Noah, close enough for us to consider a later attempt on Arken (the Ark) and with other peaks within reach. After all the hours of pulk hauling we were tired and harried by a cold wind we were glad to retreat into sleeping bags for a long rest. Sleep tempered our sense of frustration but as we discussed the situation we determined to remain at this camp for a week at least, trying to reach some summits and work out how to tackle the Ark. Indeed, we resolved to recce an approach to the Ark to be executed in the night hours to avoid the heat of the day. A missed alarm delayed our departure and a cold wind did not make for a comfortable prospect. As we pushed out a route, Willem, fit for his years but not having used skis for perhaps the last forty of them, found the icy conditions a bit demanding and opted to return to camp. After we had delivered him safely back, Paul, Robin and I went more quickly across the glacier, negotiating crevasses on the way to reach the "gutter", the ablation valley at the foot of the Ark's South Face. Here we could see a suitable location for a short stay bivouac camp and easy access onto the mountain slopes.

We returned to Camp Noah to report and make other plans. Geoff, trusty old warhorse, was eager for another climb by now, so in the evening joined with Sandy and me to ski up into the north-facing cirque below Copper Knob and Peak Bruno. From the col at its head sprang a long arête leading to a high summit at over 2,300 metres. Could we get to it? In a few hours we had forged a route up snow and ice slopes to a final exposed icy traverse into the col. To the south an impressively wide vista of huge glacier and vast icecap opened up, beyond the inner end of Gaaseland's peninsula. Immediately above us rose the problematic feature of a 75 metres high rock step, barring the way to the upper arête. This was patently impossible to climb direct – for us – and although it seemed at first feasible to thread a way across its south flank by linking ledges and snow bands, the potential track was littered with masses of loose perched blocks and rubble. After giving it all a long hard stare we baulked at the prospect of some hours of nerve-wracking passage up, and later on, down this section, so turned to go down. As Geoff said "It is decisions like this that have kept us alive and active in the mountains all of our lives."

Sagely we found our way back to camp and back into cold wind. The Ark now beckoned. The next evening we took two of the pulks to transport a couple of tents and sleeping gear, plus the required climbing equipment to go back across the glacier on our reconnoitred route to set up our advance bivouac. Seen from our 2008 Camp Venturi, the Ark looked like a very hard nut to crack, but our Twin Otter flypasts had showed us a possible route on its South Face which was now where we were in position. Willem, not a technical climber, was going to remain in the close environs of the bivouac where he was happy to spend time geologising and no doubt remembering his brother whose name graces these fabulous mountains. The rest of the group, after a period of repose, began to mount the lower slopes of the Ark, at first over blocks and scree. There was evidence that these south-facing slopes support some vegetation later in the season – mosses, lichens, some grasses and flowers – and we were cheered to see a few Ptarmigan and Snow Buntings. We even came across a large hairy caterpillar close to some house-sized boulders.

After just over an hour we set foot on the Great Snow Terrace which stretches across more than 2 kilometres of the face. We made rapid progress across the first half of this to a point where we needed to rope up and begin to use crampons. The far eastern end of the Terrace ran into a feeder slope descending steeply from the glacier which drapes the upper eastern shelf of the Ark, the "aft deck" so to speak. Further across to the right, but no threat to our route, the glacier reaches the cliff edge in a mighty serac barrier, with many immense sections slowly working their way to a gravity and melt-induced collapse. Our own optimism at our progress was now sorely tried. The remainder of the Terrace, although not technically difficult, carried an eggshell-like layer of surface crust. Unluckily for us this crust proved on this night to be non-weightbearing for more than a step or two together, and at each breakage, I, as the man in front was plunged through into often crotch-deep snow of a sugarlike consistency. A trench had to be trampled into this stuff, hardly even consolidating for those following.

Forward movement slowed to a funereal pace, with much breath-sapping effort required to push out the route. This cost us time measured in hours and it was with heartfelt relief that I mounted the final steep slope leading up to the glacier shelf. During this time a splendid cloud inversion had formed, as moist air from the coast crept along the glaciers below us, leaving all the peaks and ourselves floating above this sea of fog in glorious sunshine. The glacier too, was in poor condition, with crevasses complicating our progression. We floundered in deep soft snow and our attempts to gain the rocks of the final ridge foundered. We fought mentally, between ambition and prudent judgement as we fought the snow physically. Already we were way beyond our estimate of time needed for ascent and descent, and we could see that the last stretches of ridge carried very large cornices and snow mushrooms. Prudence won out, but it was with great reluctance that the decision to renounce our climb was reached. We had unlocked the way to the summit and had made a very spirited attempt to well over 2,000 metres. We turned to start going down, the final prize remaining unclaimed. Our "If onlys…" revolved round the purgatorical condition of the Great Snow Terrace, and in truth we were very downcast.

Very tired we rejoined Willem at the bivouac camp, very thirsty and hungry, and after these needs had been met we crawled wearily into sleeping bags to rest. The hours passed and we waited for the cool shade of late evening before we recrossed the glacier back to Camp Noah with more crevasses making themselves apparent as the sun depleted the surface snow. For Robin, a very accomplished Nordic skier, all this roped-up skiing and crevasse negotiating was an added extra dimension to his range of experience. Back at Camp Noah we found some fantastic ice crystal growths, formed in the freezing air of the inversion period, fragile beauty on a macro scale but at home in this wide landscape.

After further rest, Geoff and I were champing at the bit somewhat for a decent summit. Paul and Robin left with Willem for an ascent of Copper Knob by a different route to allow our Swiss-Dutch friend to see from a mountain top some more of the terrain studied by his brother all those years ago. Sandy decided that Geoff and I would go more quickly as a pair so she waved us off as we set out in evening sunshine. Directly above our camp rose the imposing bulk of Bændelbjerg, named by geologists for the striped, tape-like rockbands exposed on its west face ("bændel = tape: Danish-English). We had been studying the North West Ridge for some days, plotting a potential route up its almost 900 metres of height-gain. It is a very beautiful mountain. A short approach on skis took us just past the foot of the ridge. From here we climbed up a couloir cutting through the lowest rocks to exit via a sort of gateway onto a snowfield which allowed access onto the main ridge crest. As we climbed we could see Paul, Willem and Robin on their way back to camp, but soon afterwards we noticed that once again fog was creeping up the glacier. From below it probably looked like the arrival of bad weather and we later learned that the others had expected us to turn back.

From our own position on the mountain we were above the fog, and although the sky clouded up we felt it was fine enough to press on. There was no wind. As the intricacies of the route unwound we placed a cairn or two as markers to guide our descent. A mix of snow and easy rock scrambling led us up the ridge towards where larger rockbands intersected the crest. After a section of traversing movement we arrived beneath the most awkward-looking one. A brief foray out left onto the exposed North Face via rather fragile ice proved to be a misleading avenue of progress. Direct it would have to be, and this would obviously be the crux of the climb. If a way could be forced the summit could be reached. Geoff set up a solid belay anchor and adopted his reassuring

Hauling pulks to move camp below Bændelbjerg, Paul Stern Land

Bændelbjerg, first ascent by Cloudspotter's Ridge, rising L to R parallel to left skyline

positive attitude of support and encouragement. Above rose a groove, upholstered with ice and a few blocks. These turned out to be well-fixed and I was able to move up and right. The next section would be make or break. After fixing a sound running belay I moved up to below a set of jutting overlaps to set foot onto a large flake. Here I needed to take off my gloves, but decided to try it still wearing crampons. To move up and right would lead to a smooth holdless slab; the overlaps would have to be taken head-on. Grasping the rocks, my rucksack tugging me backwards, I carefully placed my crampon points onto the top of the flake then pulled mightily. Straightening up I could reach beyond the next overlap to some flat holds and moved my feet further up the wall willing the steel points to stay. A few loose rocks had to be cast away into the depths below then a few more muscular pulls took me past the difficult passage. After another few metres I reached a stance where I could fix a good belay anchor to safeguard Geoff as he followed.

Wily old mountaineer that he is, Geoff found a way to bridge up some of this crux section to join me, and from there we felt confident of completing our route. The "Bonatti Pitch" was a nice piece of quite difficult climbing and was the key to our ascent. Geoff led on through a varied section of snow, ice and rock then we went up to a final steepening of ice by a thin rockband to get onto what turned into the summit slopes. Some light snow was now falling as we mounted the upper part of the peak. Above us the sky brightened and opened up, and as we went on we found our way along and up an exposed curving crest, falling convex to the left and curling over to the right into stupendous cornices. We kept well back from this edge on a mixture of ice and windslab snow until there was no more uphill to go up. We had won the first ascent to the 2,341 metres summit of Bændelbjerg. With wide grins we looked about us, across all the other peaks of Paul Stern Land, appearing from and vanishing into the mists. The Ark showed its long crest over to the north. Ararat lay in the northwest. Cameras were brought into play, not in very good light, but a record was made.

After we had caught our breaths, we knew, as veteran alpinists and Greenland old hands, that you don't toast success until you're safely back down, so we turned our attention to that task. Confident and trusting in each other's skills we left the summit – no rocks for any cairn there – and outflanked the corniced edge. Quickly we lost height, climbing down with an occasional running belay between us. More awkward sections caused us to slow at times, but in time we reached a marker cairn above the Bonatti Pitch. Here we rigged up an abseil point, to decend by sliding down the rope, double checking everything for security. The rope pulled down without a hitch and we resumed the down climbing. Much lower down we stopped to drink at a wonderful natural bivouac niche formed by a beautifully curved section of rock arching into a roof over an ample two-man sized ledge seat. Then on down, picking out more of our markers to find the top of the long initial couloir. After coming down this we hopped over two or three crevasses and stomped down to where we'd left our skis.

In just over a half-hour we were gliding back into camp, to the relief of our friends, having been on the go for about fourteen hours. Then we could celebrate our first ascent of Bændelbjerg, 2,341 metres, via the Cloudspotter's Ridge (North West) as Geoff named it. We both felt it ranked amongst the best we have done in Greenland. The overnight mists had cleared leaving colder but sunny weather. Geoff and I needed to sleep for some time but in the evening we all packed up to move back up the glacier to our original camp area. Here the wind began to reassert itself and we decided to stay put for at least one more night. This gave Geoff and me time to recover in a more dignified manner, as the wind hammered and rattled the tents for hours on end. As a group we now planned to move camp once again, heading further northwest for about 5 kilometres to get nearer to Ararat, the highest mountain in the area. Athough Sandy, Geoff and I had already claimed the first ascent of this peak in 2008, the others wanted to climb it too, and we felt there was a good way to make a full traverse of it by descending a new route so we concurred with their wishes. A new camp would also put us in reach of a high nunatak ridge right on the fringe of the Inland Ice so we had an added incentive.

During an afternoon we moved away to the northwest, finding easier travel on the now colder, firmer surfaces. After just over 5 kilometres and having gained 100 metres of height, we set up a new camp with a stunning 360 degree view encompassing most of Paul Stern Land and sweeping sections of the Inland Ice with several sentry nunataks. As this location was not too distant from our last camp site of 2008, I suspected that sooner or later the windspill from the icecap would kick in to temper our idyll. Then we'd had Camp Venturi; now we were to spend a few days at "Camp Katabat". We'd got the camp set up during a warm, calm spell, but this flattered to deceive. As we retired for the night the wind blew in, redoubled its efforts and howled with a vengeance all night long. Sleep became intermittent.

The morning was too cold for activity so we waited for the wind to abate. By early afternoon we could leave Camp Katabat and directed our skis towards Ararat. It was not long before we began to encounter crevasses, but most of them were narrow and easy to cross. At one point though, suspicious of a snowbridge, I gave it a good whack with a ski pole whereon a big section dropped straight in to reveal a deep, deep chamber at least two metres across! This was a serious crevasse calling for a retreat and a change of direction. The grid of crevasses became more closely spaced but we won through to the gutter at the mountain foot to begin our climb. We could start unroped until well on the way to the col between Ararat and Peak Emyr, another of our 2008 peaks. Willem again opted for a few hours of geology while the rest of us climbed. Taking a diagonal line across the base of Emyr, we remarked how the rocks here bore no trace of vegetation unlike on the Ark.

From a height of 2,000 metres we followed the route along Ararat's West Ridge which we had pioneered in 2008 and the firm snow and ice allowed us to move very quickly. Approaching the corniced edge of the summit ridge, the formation seemed a little different to that of two years ago but we crossed it easily. The wide view over the northern nunataks and Saven Range opened out before us and we moved along the back of the cornice to the summit of Ararat in just a few minutes. Our little cairn still stood on the topmost rock just a metre or so down, proof of our first visit. Here were two of the first ascent party now making the second ascent too. We gazed around us, reminding ourselves of what we'd seen before in the middle of a cold night. Now we were in the warmth of a late afternoon. Ararat commands a fine view of the north face of the Ark, where a very long ice face could perhaps be climbed. But its foot meets a very tortured glacier, riddled with complex crevasses, moraine bands and rivers of meltwater even at this time in late spring. Maybe the crux there would be just reaching the base of the climb?

Conscious of Willem waiting for us below, we left the summit to go off down the South East Ridge of Ararat to effect our first traverse. The ridge became more and more photogenic as we went down it, so there was plenty of camerawork to do as variegated cornice shapes succeeded one another. At a suitable point we struck off to the right on a long, long diagonal line down the huge snowfield of the South West Face. This gave a very rapid descent until the snow petered out into boulderfields. We picked our way through these, crossing odd snow patches, in one of which we discovered fresh footprints made by an Arctic Fox, until we made a rendezvous with the patient Willem. We soon finished the descent to the skis in the ablation hollow and re-roped to cross the glacier back to Camp Katabat. The crevasse numbers seemed to have multiplied by the day and we were glad to regain the safe area round the tents, and by midnight we were ready for sleep. The following day we spent some time in discussion over our exit stategy – and tossed around ideas for future Arctic expeditions.

Robin, primarily a ski tourer, particularly wanted to visit the nunatak zone out by the Inland Ice so we arranged that for our final mountain outing we would try to get to one of the highest unclimbed ones the next day. This would not be a very technical ascent so we could spare ourselves the weight of most climbing equipment apart from that needed to cope with any potential crevasse incident. Thus, Sandy, Robin and I set out from camp to try to quickly ski the several kilometres out to the west. We were delayed for a while by a breakage and failure in one of my ski bindings, but a little ingenuity with a length of cord and some medical tape from a first aid kit allowed a jury-rigged repair so we could continue our approach. Once out by the nunatak, having crossed a number of crevasses on the way, we went easily on foot up a ridge of snow and some loose rock to the domed summit at 2,090 metres from where we could let Robin try to take in the sheer scale of the Inland Ice, looking around over what can seem like a white ocean. Just a few metres from the highest point was an outcropping of rock where we soon erected a tall cairn.

Sandy and I chose to dedicate this first ascent to one of our dear friends in Norway who has extended many kindnesses to us over the years, thus Solbjørgs Fjell. Our line of ascent and descent we called "Cryoconite Ridge" – a term coined by the explorer Nordenskiöld to represent all the accumulated debris that icecaps and glaciers collect and encapsulate; atmospheric soot, dust and other particles, pollen grains, wind-blown rock flour and the like, all of which add to the atmospheric and climatic record. During our own stay we had been noticing the seeming increase in particulate matter released into our snowmelt water supply and surface contamination as the seasonal melt progressed.

Our return to Camp Katabat was rapid, my binding repair proving adequate to the job. When we got back Paul remarked that the camp had been visited during the day by a large, heavy-looking Raven, which reappeared later in the evening to flap around for a while. We rested very well, Robin pleased with his outing. The next morning, in leisurely fashion we packed up and started our move back down the glacier to

the landing zone depot. This was easy skiing so only took two or three hours, but as we might have suspected yet more crevasses were noticed as the melt-out continued. Some of these fissures were awkwardly in our line of travel, but none of them were overly wide so just a few small detours were needed. As we neared the depot area we could see the Raven again, on the ground. It flapped away heavily as we grew close and then we became aware of its depredations over what must have been several visits during our absence. Despite our care in securing the depot, the big black bird had spent some time over the last few days in raiding our food supply, scattering debris far and wide and making far more mess than one would credit to just one creature. As well as litter there were copious amounts of droppings as a result of the bird's gluttonous bonanza. After we had probed out a safe new area for our tents we repitched our camp then spent quite a lot of time picking up all the scattered garbage and damaged food items to restore the site to our own standards of assiduous "light tread" cleanlinesss.

Sooner or later, all expeditions come to an end

Later on, having arranged for our next day aircraft pick-up via a satellite 'phonecall we packed up the bulk of of our equipment and still found time to relive some of our recent experiences, and put our near misses into perspective. After a final night of restful sleep the last packing was completed and we waited for the Twin Otter to arrive. In view of the amount of melt-out and the prevalence of crevasses, Paul and I sought out and marked the best landing line for the skiplane – one with the least bumps and only a couple of minor crevasses. We set a windsock at the critical touchdown point and resumed our wait in the bright sunshine. Some fifteen minutes in advance of the expected time we heard the familiar engine noise and very soon the red-painted aeroplane flashed into view to make a low pass to inspect the marked strip. A couple of quick turns to line up the approach followed, then a pinpoint touchdown by the windsock and a rapid slowdown to a halt. A short taxi run positioned the aircraft for take-off, then we were busy with loading.

Once this was all done, in less than an hour, we persuaded the pilots once in the air to make a close flyaround of the summit of the Ark to give us a near view of the final section on the way out. The hard snow surface allowed a take-off run of just thirty seconds before getting airborne and just a few minutes later we circled the top of the Ark. Our own tracks were still visible in the snows, together with one fresh avalanche trail. We could clearly see that had conditions been just a little more in our favour we could have reached the summit without much more difficulty. Looking across to the heartland of Paul Stern Land, we felt that helicopter access might be the only sure way to get right to the ideal location for a central camp. This would probably be prohibitively expensive. But those bright shining mountains are still there, and the Ark sails serenely on its sea of glaciers. Who knows if others may at some time find a way to go beyond the signposts we have established?

We flew out to the east, crossing vast tracts of impressive landscape, many parts suggesting future exciting expedition prospects. Out to Constable Pynt, then on again over the ocean to Akureyri in northern Iceland, and in time to our repective homelands. Will we return to this wonderful Arctic to continue our love affair with this fabulous landscape treasure? For sure some of us will dream of it, and some of us will strain our sinews to make it happen.

As Thoreau puts it – "Dreams are the touchstones of our characters… In wildness is the preservation of the world."

2008 EXPEDITION TO PAUL STERN LAND, NORTHEAST GREENLAND
Geoff Bonney, Sandy Gregson and Jim Gregson

2010 EXPEDITION TO PAUL STERN LAND, NORTHEAST GREENLAND
Robin Collins, Willem-B. Stern, Paul Walker, Geoff Bonney, Sandy Gregson and Jim Gregson

Appendix 1

The Development of Mountaineering in East and Northeast Greenland – An Outline History

Most early expeditions to Greenland had scientific rather than mountaineering objectives. Nevertheless there was considerable exploration and discovery of mountain ranges and a number of ascents were made, perhaps the earliest being J. Payer's 1870 climb of Payer Spitze, 2,133 metres, above Kejser Franz-Joseph Fjord. Further interest in Greenland was catalysed by Nansen's first crossing of the Inland Ice in 1888.

A number of other routes crossing the icecap were pioneered at the end of the 19th Century and the start of the 20th. Significantly for future mountaineering, the Swiss Alfred de Quervain's west to east crossing party discovered and named the Schweizerland area for its array of Alpine peaks reminiscent of their homeland. This was in 1912. The Scottish explorer J.M. Wordie led teams into northeast Greenland in 1926 and 1929, in the latter year making the first ascent of Petermanns Bjerg, the highest mountain in the High Arctic and once thought to be the loftiest in all Greenland.

The decade of the 1930s saw a surge of interest in Greenland's mountains. Between 1930 and 1932 the Gino Watkins-led British Arctic Air Route Expedition travelled extensively on the Inland Ice and in the east coast mountains. Attempts were made on Mont Forel, and aerial survey flights led to the discovery of what later were named the Watkins Bjerge where the highest peaks on the whole island stood. In 1933 Miss Louise Boyd's American Expedition made a number of ascents to the north of Petermanns Bjerg. More important discoveries were accomplished by Martin Lindsay's British Trans-Greenland Expedition which in 1934 crossed the Inland Ice from west to east to fix the position of "The Monarch",

later renamed Gunnbjørns Fjeld, confirming its primacy of altitude. Lindsay then sledged hundreds of kilometres southwest to Ammassalik discovering en route the extensive ranges of the Kronprins Frederik Bjerge.

In 1935, Lawrence Wager who had been a member of Watkins's expedition returned to the icebound east coast to pioneer a route inland to make the first ascent of Gunnbjørns Fjeld, ca.3,700 metres, as well as sighting the Lemon Bjerge to the northeast of Kangerdlugssuaq Fjord. During 1938 a Swiss expedition including André Roch travelled through Schweizerland to make the first ascent of Mont Forel, 3,600 metres, and thirteen other significant firsts, including Laupers Bjerg, Rødebjerg and Rytterknaegten, drawing attention to the wealth of fine peaks in this district.

The post-World War Two years heralded an increasing rate of visits to East and Northeast Greenland as awareness of mountaineering possibilities grew. Lauge Koch's series of East Greenland Expeditions from 1950 to 1953, although scientific in intent, numbered keen and capable mountaineers among its personnel, notably J. Haller and W. Diehl, who climbed many important peaks in Goodenough Land, Suess Land and other districts of Christian X Land. The ascents of Lauge Kochs Bjerg, Payers Tinde, Hamlet Bjerg, Shackletons Bjerg and Pluto Nunatak date from this period. More northerly still, the Barth Mountains and Dronning Louise Land were also the setting for pioneer ascents by the British North Greenland Expedition. The 1950s also saw the start of what became prolific development of mountaineering in the spectacular ranges of the Staunings Alps. Expeditions from Norway, Switzerland, Denmark, Austria and Scotland made large numbers of first ascents.

In 1954 Haller and Diehl seized their opportunity to be the first to climb Danmarkstinde (Dansketinde), the highest peak in the Staunings, 2,930 metres, and repeated the climb of Norsketinde (Stortoppen) soon after its first ascent by Norwegians and Danes. Many more expeditions followed into the Staunings Alps throughout the 1960s with teams from many nations making multiple first ascents in this very attractive area.

The mountains of the Ammassalik region, Schweizerland and areas near to Mont Forel also continued to draw in expeditions, with extensive achievements through the 1960s by teams from Japan, Switzerland, Sweden and Great Britain. On a sadder note, the first fatalities in Greenland's mountains befell the 1966 (British) Royal Navy Expedition which lost two members in separate accidents. The 1963 Scottish East Greenland Expedition led by P. Gribbon climbed extensively in "Caledonia" adjacent to Schweizerland, and the Swiss under S. Angerer in 1966 climbed some very impressive peaks from the glaciers extending northeast of the huge Glacier de France.

As the decade of the 1960s closed and moved into its successor 1970s, the numbers of expeditions with mountaineering ambitions also grew. However, the majority of them continued to visit areas already known, leading to more intensive development with some notable increases in technical climbing standards rather than exploration of new regions. Improved access by air, most importantly via the airstrip at Kulusuk on the east coast began to make significant differences, although there were still a number of fine initiatives made by sea-borne approaches. The European nations were at the forefront of the development of mountaineering with many groups originating from Italy, France, Germany and Great Britain. The Staunings Alps continued to draw attention and there was a renewal of interest into the considerable possibilities of the Kronprins Frederik Bjerge. The high peaks in the vicinity of Mont Forel were a magnet for some but others sought out difficulty elsewhere, such as the Swiss ascents of the Eisdom, the Istinde and the Eismeer Jungfrau near the Pourquoi-pas Glacier in 1966, and the Croatians on Ingolffjeld in 1971. Further north a few groups attempted to open up the harder to reach unknown regions behind the Blosseville Coast and areas adjacent to Scoresbysund.

Interest was encouraged at this time by the publication of two important sources of information. Mario Fantin published his major work in Italian: *Montagne di Groenlandia* tried to cover a full account of all expeditions to Greenland up to 1969. In 1971, Donald Bennet's *Staunings Alps* chronicled the intensive development of that region. During the summer of 1970, Andrew Ross's expedition sailed by open boat all the way from Scoresbysund to Wiedemanns Fjord then trekked inland to succeed on the challenging first ascent of Ejnar Mikkelsens Fjeld, a major prize. In 1972 Gunnbjørns Fjeld received only its second ascent by Alastair Allan's British-Danish team and in the eastern sector of the Watkins Bjerge, Brown and Soper from Britain's Sheffield University climbed the high Borgtinde for the first time. Another British group began to open up the Roscoe Bjerge in Liverpool Land. Another important initiative occurred in 1972. The Westminster East Greenland Expedition including Stan Woolley sailed from Kulusuk to Kangerdlugssuaq Fjord and once landed, explored the Frederiksbjorg Glacier into the Lemon Bjerge, drawing attention to these exciting Alpine ranges first seen by Wager in 1935. Woolley was also instrumental in subsequent years in opening up other areas, most importantly the difficult to reach northerly parts of the Kronprins Frederik Bjerge. All through the later 1970s and 1980s expedition numbers grew, with much more intensive development in districts where it was known that good mountaineering objectives proliferated, including many ascents of new routes on peaks already climbed.

As access to Greenland's eastern and northeastern mountains has always been problematic, a far-reaching change in the 1980s was to give a very important impetus to Arctic mountaineering. This was the start of icecap and glacier landings by ski-equipped aircraft. Such approaches began in 1988 in the Watkins Bjerge marking the long association of skilful Icelandic pilots with mountaineering expeditions. The first flights were made into the Watkins Bjerge eliminating the time-consuming overland approaches and led to a surge of interest in the mountains surrounding Gunnbjørns Fjeld, as well as popularising ascents of this highest of Greenland's summits. It soon became clear that ten or more of the loftiest Arctic mountains were clustered in this region. In 1988 the British team including Jim Lowther and Lewis Jones climbed Gunnbjørns Fjeld, the Cone and the Dome, disproving earlier claims that these latter two exceeded the former in height. The Cone and Dome were later officially renamed as Qaqqaq Johnson and Qaqqaq Kershaw and measured as Greenland's third and second highest mountains. Also in 1988 a Swedish group led by Bengt Rodin succeeded in climbing both Gunnbjørns Fjeld and Mont Forel during the same expedition by making the huge ski journey between the two peaks.

As the 1980s gave way to the 1990s, the popularity of the mountains of East Greenland escalated, despite the continuing high levels of expense involved in getting there. Regions like the Staunings Alps, the Lemon Bjerge and Schweizerland where good quality rock-climbing and technical mountaineering are in plentiful supply drew in more mountaineers each year. Helicopter and skiplane access made it easier to get quickly into the heart of the ranges, even allowing for the at times inevitable bad weather delays. Interest in the highest summits has also maintained a steady stream of suitors, and guided parties have become regular, particularly to Gunnbjørns Fjeld, which normally receives between two and four ascents each season. In 1998 a Swiss team of four led by Roland Aeschimann, made the second ascent of Ejnar Mikkelsens Fjeld by a repeat of the south glacier approach, probably the single most impressive Alpine peak in the whole of Greenland with faces on three sides rising some 2,000 metres fom the Kronborg Glacier. This was followed in 2000 by the second ascent of its close neighbour Borgtinde by a Tangent group led by Nigel Edwards, along with several other first ascents in the region. Tragically at this time, a nearby peak was the site of the death of a nephew of the well-known Dutch climber Ronald Naar in a crevasse fall during a ski descent in poor visibility. There has also been an increasing level of interest in the development of new areas, especially by groups from Great Britain. This has resulted in much more travel, exploration and ascents in the Kronprins Frederik Bjerge, the many peaks round the Kangerdlussuaq Basin, the Watkins Bjerge, and areas behind the Blosseville Coast such as the Rignys Bjerg mountains, the Lindbergh Fjelde, the Gronau Nunatakker, the mountains of Knud Rasmussen Land and the remote peaks of the aptly named Camp Icefield. Further north still, within the Greenland National Park area, more British groups have been very active climbing in Goodenough Land, Louise Boyds Land, the Martin Knudsens and Niel Holgersens Nunatakker and Dronning Louise Land. A major factor in these recent developments since the early 1990s has been the role of Paul Walker and his logistics operation, Tangent Expeditions International, which by co-ordination of air operations has facilitated access for many expeditions into these more remote areas during the later 1990s and 2000s. Further south, the Schweizerland region is still a major draw with continuing development of high-standard rock-climbing, and increasingly the seeking out of big wall climbing as seen in the Fox Jaw Cirque above Tasiilaq Fjord, and on prominent peaks like Tupilak by the September 16 Glacier. The Staunings Alps too, go on attracting those seeking demanding Alpine climbing, and there are exciting developments involving excellent rock climbing prospects in Milne Land and neighbouring Renland following recent discoveries. These trends seem likely to persist, alongside a growing interest in ski-touring and ski-mountaineering. The last few years have also seen the first signs of development of winter mountaineering in Greenland, an exciting and challenging prospect. In March 2004 Paul Walker led an international team of climbers who attempted the first ever winter ascent of Gunnbjørns Fjeld. Forced back by temperatures in the minus 40s Celsius with strong winds and fierce windchill. A return was made in the winter of 2006 when a successful ascent was completed and other peaks are likely to attract those who will not be daunted by harsh cold conditions. Thus, although Greenland's many and varied mountains lack the altitude of the Himalaya or the Andes, their remoteness and likeness to Antarctica, and the promise of new ascents will go on attracting those who search for the rewards of exploration and attainment of new mountaineering experiences as the 21st Century marches on.

REFERENCE SOURCES

1 Mountaineering in Greenland 1870-1966: The Mountain World 1966-1967: Swiss Foundation for Alpine Research
2 Mountaineering in Greenland 1967-1976: The American Alpine Journal 1979: American Alpine Club
3 Mountaineering in Greenland 1977-1986: The American Alpine Journal 1988: American Alpine club. (The American Alpine Journal published annually continues to be the most comprehensive source of information and reports of mountaineering in Greenland)
4 Montagne di Groenlandia: Mario Fantin: Tamari Editori, Bologna 1969.
5 Sea, Ice and Rock: Christian Bonington and Robin Knox- Johnston: Hodder and Stoughton, London 1992
6 Greenland Ventures: Stan Woolley: Athena Press, London 2004
7 Tangent Expeditions International archive: *www.climbgreenland.com*

Appendix 2

List of Mountain Ascents

(Geodetic Reference WGS84 – Position Coordinates Lat. Long.)

CHAPTER 1   SCHWEIZERLAND 1991
ASCENTS

Peak 1   Dragon Peak c.1800m – west of Slangen Pass – N66.14 W36.40

Peak 2   P1720m – 16 September Glacier – N66.17 W36.27

Peak 3   c.1700m – N66.18 W36.30

Peak 4   Slangen East Peak c.1900m – N66.13 W36.35

Peak 5   c.1700m – N66.12 W36.40 (also attempted – P2070 – N66.20 W36.22)

CHAPTER 4   POURQUOI-PAS GLACIER 1994
ASCENTS

Peak 1   c.1500m – N66.37 W35.43 – 1st ascent (E Ridge) 25/07/94

Peak 2   c.2200m – N66.42 W35.50 – 1st ascent (NW Ridge) 28/07/94

Peak 3   c.2100m – N66.43 W35.46 – 1st ascent (N Ridge) 29/07/94

Peak 4   c.2180m – N66.43 W35.44 – 1st ascent (NE Ridge) 30/07/94

Peak 5   c.2080m – N66.43 W35.47 – 1st ascent (E Face) 31/07/94

Peak 6   c.2000m – N66.42 W35.53 – 1st ascent (N Flank) 31/07/94

Peak 7   c.2000m – N66.42 W35.52 – 1st ascent (N Flank) 31/07/94

Peak 8   c.2090m – N66.40 W35.34 – 1st British ascent 05/08/94
             (Swiss note found in cairn)

Peak 9   c.1650m – N66.41 W35.32 – 1st ascent (W Ridge/S Face) 10/08/94

Peak 10 c.2400m – N66.40 W35.31 – 1st British ascent (W Flank/NE Ridge)
11/08/94 (cairn found)

Peak 11 c.2000m – N66.39 W35.34 – 1st ascent (NE Flank) 11/08/94

Peak 12 c.1990m – N66.39 W35.35 – 1st ascent (E Flank) 11/08/94

Peak 13 c.2370m – N66.40 W35.28 – 1st British ascent (N Ridge) 12/08/94
             (cairn found)

Peak 14 c.1800m – N66.38 W35.42 – 1st British ascent (N Ridge) 14/08/94
             (cairn found)

Note: a Swiss expedition was in this area in 1966

CHAPTER 6   KRONPRINS FREDERIK BJERGE 1996
ASCENTS

Peak 1   2800m – N67.11.467 W34.59.268 – 1st ascent

Peak 2   2720m – N67.09.936 W35.01.818 – 1st ascent

Peak 3   2780m – N67.10.883 W35.20.599 – 1st ascent

Peak 4   2725m – N67.13.035 W35.24.817 – 1st ascent

Peak 5   2630m – N67.13.014 W35.20.331 – 1st ascent

Peak 6   2975m – N67.10.343 W35.26.858 – 1st ascent

Peak 7   2750m – N67.10.613 W34.54.915 – 1st ascent

Peak 8   2640m – N67.11.009 W34.54.246 – 1st ascent

Peak 9   2440m – N67.11.125 W34.42.630 – 1st ascent (Anniversary Peak)

Peak 10 2450m – N67.09.175 W34.49.133 – 1st ascent (Laura's Peak)

Peak 11 2480m – N67.08.824 W34.50.407 – 1st ascent (Middle Peak)

Peak 12 2470m – N67.08.843 W34.50.996 – 1st ascent (West End Peak)

Peak 13 2410m – N67.13.598 W34.40.334 – 1st ascent (Nat's Peak)

Peak 14 2520m – N67.13.359 W34.40.406 – 1st ascent (White Peak)

Peak 15 2210m – N67.08.963 W34.44.406 – 1st ascent (Ridge End Peak)

Peak 16 2230m – N67.08.772 W34.43.524 – 1st ascent (Al's Peak)

Peak 17   2090m – N67.08.637 W34.41.977 – 1st ascent (End Dome Peak)
Peak 18   2550m – N67.14.859 W35.07.832 – 1st ascent (Off Map Peak)
Peak 19   2580m – N67.11.673 W35.13.583 – repeat ascent (Base Peak 1)
Peak 20   2730m – N67.12.163 W35.07.368 – repeat ascent (Base Peak 2)

Also attempted 2950m – N67.13.000 W35.18.000 – ("Crown Prince Peak" – a major unclimbed peak)

CHAPTER 8   CHAMPS-ELYSÉES GLACIER 1997
ASCENTS

Peak 1   c.2100m – N66.43.159 W35.51.830 – 1st ascent (Rim Point 1)
Peak 2   c.2100m – N66.43.041 W35.52.512 – 1st ascent (Rim Point 2)
Peak 3   c.2100m – N66.43.035 W35.52.297 – 1st ascent (Rim Point 3)
Peak 4   c.2100m – N66.43.021 W35.52.907 – 1st ascent (Rim Point 4)
Peak 5   c.2050m – N66.46.535 W35.51.289 – 1st ascent (Sphinx Peak Tail)
Peak 6   c.2080m – N66.46.395 W35.51.498 – 1st ascent (Sphinx Peak Head)
Peak 7   2420m – N66.43.724 W35.54.160 – 1st ascent (Tangent Peak)
Peak 8   c.2180m – N66.44.167 W35.52.667 – 1st ascent (Coxcomb Peak)
Peak 9   c.2400m – N66.45.199 W35.47.795 – 1st ascent
          (Parrotspitze – up via Parrot's Beak Arête, down via S fFace)
Peak 10   c.2270m – N66.43.113 W35.48.452 – 1st ascent (Hidden Peak)
Peak 11   c.2240m – N66.43.305 W35.48.701 – 1st ascent (Wellhidden Peak)

CHAPTER 10   SHACKLETONS BJERG 1998
ASCENTS

Peak 1   2450m – N72.53.414 W29.16.516 – 2nd ascent (Uranus)
Peak 2   2520m – N72.52.547 W29.15.863 – 2nd ascent (Pluto)
Peak 3   2390m – N72.54.383 W29.16.361 – 2nd ascent (Venus)
Peak 4   2400m – N72.56.246 W29.11.160 – 2nd ascent (Trio Peak)
Peak 5   2450m – N72.56.546 W29.10.438 – 1st ascent (Peeping Peak)
Peak 6   2310m – N72.54.360 W29.08.878 – 2nd ascent (Middle Peak)
Peak 7   2320m – N72.54.409 W29.08.595 – 2nd ascent (End Peak)
Peak 8   2310m – N72.54.229 W29.09.321 – 1st ascent (Wart Peak)
Peak 9   2370m – N72.54.869 W29.21.204 – 1st ascent (Simon's Peak N top)

Peak 10   2350m – N72.54.799 W29.21.276 – 1st ascent (Simon's Peak 2)
Peak 11   2360m – N72.54.702 W29.21.463 – 1st ascent (Simon's Peak 3)
Peak 12   2410m – N72.54.545 W29.21.714 – 1st ascent (Simon's Peak Main)
Peak 13   2890m – N72.53.778 W28.46.815 – 3rd ascent (Shackletons Bjerg)
Peak 14   2400m – N72.51.602 W28.46.552 – 2nd ascent (Pulk Peak)
Peak 15   2530m – N72.54.357 W28.39.929 – 2nd ascent (Echo Pond Peak)
Peak 16   2275m – N72.48.484 W28.30.409 – 1st ascent (Nevis Peak)
Peak 17   2290m – N72.48.275 W28.29.688 – 2nd ascent (Link Peak)
Peak 18   2230m – N72.50.593 W28.23.448 – 1st ascent (Banded Peak)
Peak 19   2210m – N72.50.251 W28.23.656 – 1st ascent (Rusty Point)
Peak 20   2150m – N72.50.012 W28.23.840 – 1st ascent (Pin Point)
Peak 21   2420m – N72.47.604 W28.28.653 – 1st ascent (Snow Queen Peak)
Peaks 22 – 27   c.2280m – N72.50 W28.20 – 1st ascent (6 Molars on
          Toothed Ridge Traverse)
Peak 28   2310m - N72.50.777 W28.19.582 - 1st ascent (Mørkfinger)

CHAPTER 12   WATKINS BJERGE/GUNNBJØRNS FJELD 1999
ASCENTS

Peak 1   3367m – N68.48.392 W29.16.979 – 1st ascent (Forefinger Peak)
Peak 2   3020m – N68.51.717 W29.18.857 – 1st ascent (Terra Nova Peak)
Peak 3   2960m – N68.51.682 W29.20.015 – 1st ascent (Flash Point)
Peak 4   3609m – N68.48.681 W29.33.461 – repeat ascent (Paul-Emil Victor Peak)
Peak 5   3249m – N68.51.000 W29.16.000 – 1st ascent (Midnight Peak)
Peak 6   3693m – N68.55.111 W29.53.970 – repeat ascent (Gunnbjørns Fjeld)

Also attempted: Qaqqaq Johnson and Qaqqaq Kershaw (formerly Dome and Cone)

CHAPTER 14   RIGNYS BJERG 2001
ASCENTS

Peak 1   2000m – N69.10.255 W26.41.376 – 1st ascent (Whiteliner Peak)
Peak 2   2025m – N69.09.881 W26.43.233 – 1st ascent (Centrepoint Peak)
Peak 3   2030m – N69.09.435 W26.43.148 – 1st ascent (Dumperfjeld)
Peak 4   2310m – N69.09.861 W26.54.412 – 1st ascent (Majordomo Peak)
Peak 5   2045m – N69.11.743 W26.48.478 – 1st ascent (Jack Tar Peak)

Peak 6 2340m – N69.11.546 W26.57.187 – 2nd ascent (Anchorman Peak)
Peak 7 2360m – N69.11636 W26.52.158 – 1st ascent (Narwhal Tooth Peak
via Harpoon Ridge)
Peak 8 1910m – N69.10.250 W26.46.765 – 1st ascent (Farawa Peak)

CHAPTER 18   SORTEBRÆ RANGES 2006
ASCENTS
Peak 1 2340m – N69.06.126 W27.31.877 – 1st ascent (Triangle Peak)
Peak 2 2405m – N69.04.487 W27.34.971 – 1st ascent (Surprise Peak)
Peak 3 2151m – N69.01.799 W27.34.394 – 1st ascent (Devil's Dome)
Peak 4 2285m – N69.03.366 W27.32.179 – 1st ascent (Stegosaurus 4)
Peak 5 2189m – N69.01.355 W27.33.834 – 1st ascent (The Nipple)
Peak 6 2165m – N69.04.797 W27.32.239 – 1st ascent (Snow Castle)
Peak 7 2276m – N69.03.146 W27.32.658 – 1st ascent (Stegosaurus 7)

Also two other attempts given up in unsafe conditions

CHAPTER 20   PAUL STERN LAND 2008 AND 2010
ASCENTS 2008
Peak 1 2060m – N70.24.671 W30.08.600 – 1st ascent (Nunatak Georg)
Peak 2 2180m – N70.31.991 W29.58.193 – 1st ascent (Garnet Dome)
Peak 3 2465m – N70.31.024 W29.56.471 – 1st ascent (Peak Emyr)
Peak 4 2480m – N70.30.899 W29.53.139 – 1st ascent (Ararat)
Peak 5 2085m – N70.28.505 W30.11.971 – 1st ascent (Windscoop Beacon)

ASCENTS 2010
Peak 1 1890m – N70.26.026 W29.50.832 – 1st ascent (Copper Knob)
Peak 2 2000m – N70.25.267 W29.50.859 – 1st ascent (Weisskopf)
Peak 3 2050m – N70.24.791 W29.49.983 – 1st ascent (Peak Bruno)
Peak 4 2348m – N70.28.059 W29.43.362 – highpoint reached during
attempt on The Ark (Arken) at c.2050m
Peak 5 2341m – N70.25.384 W29.46.663 – 1st ascent (Bændelbjerg)
Peak 6 2480m – N70.30.899 W29.53.139 – 2nd ascent & 1st traverse (Ararat)
Peak 7 2090m – N70.27.303 W30.08.270 – 1st ascent (Solbjørgs Fjell)

The author completes the first ascent of Coxcomb Peak *Photo: Glenn Morris*

End of August sunset in the Kronprins Frederik Bjerge

Further Selected Reading

- Axelsson, R. 2010. *Last Days of the Arctic*. London: Polarworld/Crymogea
- Bennet, D.J. 1972. *Staunings Alps-Greenland*. Reading: Gaston's Alpine Books & West Col Productions.
- Chapman, F.S. 1933. *Northern Lights*. London: Chatto and Windus.
- Chapman, F.S. 1934. *Watkins' Last Expedition*. London: Chatto and Windus.
- Christensen, N.O. & Ebbesen, H. (No date) *Angmagssalik itsak- i gamle dage*. Publikationer fra Arktisk Institut nr.1.
- Croft, A. 1991. *A Talent For Adventure*. Upton on Severn: The S.P.A.Ltd.
- Dupree, L. 2000. *Greenland Expedition – Where Ice Is Born*. Minnetonka: North Word Press.
- Fridriksson, K. 1997. *Ammassalik A Jewel In The Arctic Crown*. Hafnafjordur: Location Greenland-Iceland.
- Hallworth, R. 1966. *The Last Flowers On Earth*. Maidstone: The Angley Book Co. Ltd.
- Higgins, A.K. *Exploration History and Place Names of Northern East Greenland*. Copenhagen: Geological Survey of Denmark and Greenland Bulletin 21
- Howarth, D. 1957. *The Sledge Patrol*. London: Collins.
- Huntford, R. 1997. *Nansen*. London: Gerald Duckworth & Co. Ltd.
- Lindsay, M. 1932. *Those Greenland Days*. Edinburgh & London: William Blackwood & Sons Ltd.
- Lindsay, M. 1934. *Sledge*. London: Cassell and Company Ltd.
- Mikkelsen, P.S. 2005. *One Thousand Days With Sirius*. Cawdor: The Steading Workshop (first pub.1986 in Danish as *Tusind dage med Sirius* by Gyldendal).
- Mikkelsen, P.S. 2006. *Twin Otter-flyvning og rejser i Groenland*. Copenhagen: Aschehoug Dansk Forlag A/S.
- Mikkelsen, P.S. 2008. *North-East Greenland – 1908-60 The Trapper Era*. Cambridge: Scott Polar Research Institute, University of Cambridge (first pub. 1994 in Danish as *Nordostgroenland* 1908-60 by Dansk Polarcenter, then revised 2001 as *Nordostgroenland* 1908-60 by Aschehoug).
- Nansen, F. 1902. *The First Crossing Of Greenland*. London: Longmans, Green, and Co. (first pub.1890 in Norwegian as *Paa Ski over Groenland*).
- Reinthaler, E. & Florian, H.C. 1998. *Greenland – The Unknown East Coast Mountains*. Norway: Bryne Offset.
- Roy, I.B. 2004. *Beyond The Imaginary Gates*. Stockport: Dewi Lewis Publishing.
- Sale, R. & Oliver,T. 1991. *Arctic Odyssey*. Swindon: The Crowood Press Ltd.
- Sale, R. 2006. *A Complete Guide To Arctic Wildlife*. London: Christopher Helm/A. & C. Black Publishers Ltd.

- Sale, R. 2008. *The Arctic – The Complete Story*. London: Frances Lincoln Limited.
- Scoresby,W. 1820. *An Account Of The Arctic Regions* 2 vols. Edinburgh: Archibald Constable.
- Scott, J.M. 1935. *Gino Watkins*. London: Hodder and Stoughton.
- Scott, J.M. 1953. *Portrait Of An Ice Cap*. London: Chatto and Windus.
- Scott, J. 2008. *Dancing On Ice*. London: Old Street Publishing Ltd.
- Smith, M. 2004. *Sir James Wordie – Polar Crusader*. Edinburgh: Birlinn Limited.
- Sorge, E. 1935. *With 'Plane, Boat & Camera in Greenland*. London: Hurst and Blackett Ltd. (first pub. in German as *Mit Flugzeug, Faltboot und Filmkamera in den Eisfjorden Groenlands* by Drei Masken Verlag A.-G. Berlin).
- Staib, B. 1963. *Across Greenland In Nansen's Track*. London: George Allen & Unwin Ltd. (first pub. 1962 in Norwegian as *Nanok: Over Groenland i Nansens Spor* by Mortensens Forlag).
- Stange, R. 2005. *East Greenland In Winter*. Dortmund: Rolf Stange. (translated from the 2004 German *Wintertour in Oestgroenland*).
- Stange, R. 2005(?). *Rocks And Ice*. Dortmund: Rolf Stange. (translated from the 2003 German *Steine Und Eis*).
- Vaughan, R. 1994. *The Arctic – A History*. Stroud: Alan Sutton Publishing Limited.
- Wheeler, S. 2009. *The Magnetic North*. London: Jonathan Cape.
- Wollaston, N. 1980. *The Man On The Ice Cap*. London: Constable.

Acknowledgements

To arrive at this stage in the progress of my book project has been a lengthy process, through a large part of my life. Many people have influenced and helped me to get this far.

My wife Sandra, with whom I have shared so many adventures and experiences, has been my most reliable companion and her support has been invaluable. I trust that she has also mostly enjoyed this life-journey in the mountains.

My mother, Mary Gregson, never questioned my attachment to the outdoors. She has always encouraged me since my childhood.

Once I became involved in outdoor life, I shared many escapades with my boyhood and lifelong friend, Tony Brown. We still laugh about some of the more madcap episodes. His father, Tommy Brown, who was our Scout Leader, taught us so much about camping skills and gave us great encouragement to develop initiative and independence.

Bob Tibbett, who showed me how to become a rock-climber, was a most dependable companion. He opened my eyes to even more possibilities. Once I had become a more accomplished mountaineer I found yet more friends with whom to share wider experiences. Among them are Alan Barber who showed me the way forward in the European Alps; John and Virginia Castick with whom I have travelled and climbed in many places; Alan Payne and Gerald Carradus, both now sadly dead, who were wonderful company in the mountains.

Andrew McClay was a most patient ski instructor, who helped me to move from the stage of faltering tyro to a still-developing telemark skier. His guidance opened the way to many exciting mountain days.

Paul Walker of Tangent Expeditions International, now my very good friend of many years, has been a steady companion of many Greenland expeditions, facilitator and provider of my experiences and opportunities to visit, enjoy and learn about the Arctic. I owe a great deal to him.

A special thank you should go to all the people involved in the Twin Otter aircraft operations who have been so vital to helping our expeditions to reach their destinations. This has been a very big factor in our successes and has been masterminded firstly by Sigurður Aðalsteinsson and later by Friðrik Adólfsson. The intrepid and skilful Icelandic pilots who have flown us have included Bjarki Hjaltason, Ragnar Magnússon, Ragnar Ólafsson, Jóhann Skírnisson, Frímann Svavarsson, Davið Jóhannson plus an equal number of copilots over the years. All of them have impressed us with their expertise and their willingness to accommodate our needs and wishes

As to my writing, I thank the various editors of the Karabiner MC Newsletter and Journals, the Hon Editors of *The Alpine Journal*, and the editors of the *American Alpine Journal*, Geoff Birtles the former editor of *High Mountain Sports*, and Barry Imeson of *Loose Scree*. All of these have at various times accepted my articles, reports and photographs and seen them through into print. To all of them I am grateful for their support and confidence in me. A particular thank you is due to John Beatty for so generously agreeing to write the foreword.

As regards this book, I am very much indebted to Vertebrate Graphics in the persons of Jon Barton and Jane Beagley. Huge thanks to them for their belief in and support of the project. They have been immensely helpful towards finalising a long-gestating scheme. Any errors in this book are my responsibility.

I hope the reader can gain some sense of the special nature of Greenland and the Arctic from these pages, and a glimpse of understanding why such wild places are important in a world so overdeveloped in other areas. I look forward to further adventures in similar vein in years still to come and hope that as you turn the pages you will, even in a vicarious way, respond to these "Echoes".

Jim Gregson
June 2012

NOTE ON PHOTOGRAPHY
The photographs in this book were made using Kodachrome transparency film, until its regretted discontinuation forced a switch to Fuji Velvia stock. I hope they help to convey my great good fortune in seeing these scenes with the direct naked eye. Cameras and lenses? – just tools to help fix them.

The author hauling a heavy load *Photo: Paul Walker*

About the Author

JIM GREGSON had a lengthy career as a schoolteacher, and throughout his life an even longer (and continuing) avocation as an alpinist and ski mountaineer. He has walked and climbed extensively in the mountains of Britain and very widely across the European Alps and Pyrenees. He is also a frequent traveller to the mountains of Norway as a telemark-style ski mountaineer.

As the pages of *Exploring Greenland* reveal, he has also made many expeditions to Greenland, making many first ascents of unclimbed peaks and ranking amongst Britain's most experienced Arctic mountaineers. He is also a prolific photographer. His writing and pictures have appeared in numerous magazines and in the prestigious pages of *The Alpine Journal* and the *American Alpine Journal*.